The Spokane Killer

The Life of Serial Killer Robert Lee Yates Jr.

Jack Smith

Copyrights

All rights reserved. © Jack Smith and Maplewood Publishing No part of this publication or the information in it may be quoted from or reproduced in any form by means such as printing, scanning, photocopying, or otherwise without prior written permission of the copyright holder.

Disclaimer and Terms of Use

Effort has been made to ensure that the information in this book is accurate and complete. However, the author and the publisher do not warrant the accuracy of the information, text, and graphics contained within the book due to the rapidly changing nature of science, research, known and unknown facts, and internet. The author and the publisher do not hold any responsibility for errors, omissions, or contrary interpretation of the subject matter herein. This book is presented solely for motivational and informational purposes only. The publisher and author of this book does not control or direct users' actions and are not responsible for the information or content shared, harm and/or action of the book readers. The presentation of the information is without contract or any type of guarantee assurance. This book is not meant to be used, nor should it be used, to diagnose or treat any medical condition. For diagnosis or treatment of any medical problem, consult your own physician. The publisher and author are not responsible for any specific health or allergy needs that may require medical supervision and are not liable for any damages or negative consequences from any treatment, action, application or preparation, to any person reading or following the information in this book. References, if any, are provided for informational purposes only and do not constitute endorsement of any websites or other sources. Readers should be aware that the websites listed in this book, if any, may change.

ISBN: 978-1539532910

Printed in the United States

Contents

Introduction 1
Before the Storm 3
In the Beginning 11
Finding a Body 25
An Investigation 33
The Next Wave 43
Another Death 53
A Mounting Investigation 63
A Dead End 73
A Living Witness 79
Conclusion 89
Further Reading 91
More Books from Jack Smith 93

Introduction

The United States of America is a complicated country. Home to many of the world's best-loved cultural icons and achievements, the nation also has a darker side. With one of the highest murder rates per capita in the so-called developed world, the country has played home to some of the most violent deaths in recorded memory. Out of this spectrum of death emerges a very specific subset of criminals: the serial killers. More than any other country, America is home to a high number of mass murderers who have moved beyond the pale of regular morality.

In this book, we will examine the life and crimes of Robert Lee Yates. Though he might not be as well known as many of the country's other serial killers, his violent crimes nevertheless left a savage impact. A veteran of the United States Army, he retired from the military and turned his penchant for violence to another end. In this book, we will attempt to discover why he made such a switch. What prompted a veteran and family man to start murdering women later in his life?

In the record books, Yates is linked with the murders of sixteen victims. The majority of these victims were female sex workers, people who operated on the fringes of society, part of an ignored and disenfranchised underworld that Yates plunged into. For two years, in the Washington area, one man was able to carry out a campaign of vicious murder, leaving a trail of bodies in his wake. This is the story of Robert Lee Yates, the family he left behind, and the women he killed. It should be noted at this juncture that several names might have been changed to preserve the privacy of their real counterparts. Every action in the story, however, is true.

Before the Storm

In order to properly prepare ourselves for this story, we should travel back to the year 1975. In the northwestern corner of the United States, in a town named Walla Walla, two young people went missing. Patrick Oliver was twenty-one and Susan Savage was twenty-two. It was the summer and the two childhood friends were happy to have seen one another after a long time apart. To celebrate, they decided to go for a picnic in one of Washington's myriad parks.

The last time anyone saw them alive was on the 13th of July at almost exactly 2:15 in the afternoon. Driving his Mercury Cougar, Patrick picked up Susan from her home and drove the two of them out into the countryside. They told their parents they would be home for dinner. As the hours dragged by, both sets of parents grew increasingly concerned.

There could have been many reasons why the two did not arrive back at the agreed time. They might have been stuck in traffic, they might have had a mechanical issue with the car, or they might simply have been having a great time and decided that there were worse things to do than spend a summer's evening in the company of an old friend. But as the sun set and the night fell, people began to worry more and more.

For Patrick's family, the concern was immediately more palpable. Patrick had an older brother, named James, who had been killed in a car accident eight years before. James had been driving his car on the 4th of July, 1967, when he lost control of the vehicle and collided with a tree. He was eighteen at the time. Dan, Patrick's other brother, was also in the car at the time. While James had been killed immediately, Dan had to spend a long time in hospital. Though he might have physically recovered, the Oliver family never truly healed from the loss of James. His death left an emotional scar. When Patrick and Susan didn't return in 1975, those old wounds were reopened.

It's no surprise the worried family started to investigate what might be happening. This meant calls to the police, calls to the local hospitals, and calls to anyone who might know the whereabouts of the two missing people. No one had anything to report. To make matters worse, Patrick and Susan hadn't left any indication where they might be going. But one of the family members managed to put together an idea that could be helpful. The two hadn't seen one another in a long time. Therefore, they might well be going to a spot that had a lot of meaning for them. A specific recreational area was mentioned, a place where the two had shared some memories in the past. The spot, east of Walla Walla and out near Wickersham Bridge, had been a frequent destination. The family decided to pay it a visit.

Patrick and Susan had been inseparable in their youth. Rather than being lovers, however, the two shared a seemingly deeper, platonic bond. Great friends growing up, they had supported one another constantly throughout the years. Susan had trained to be a designer and Patrick had been working towards a medical degree. This work meant Patrick had been offered the opportunity to study abroad in Paris for a year, a chance he seized with relish. By the summer of 1975, Patrick had completed his year abroad and had returned to Washington. His first thought had been to reunite with his old friend and this had prompted the pair's decision to venture out into the countryside.

As such, Patrick's aunt reasoned, the two might decide that a picnic spot they had shared together many years ago would be a suitable place to go. Patrick's father gathered together some people and set off to investigate the hunch. It wasn't long before they spotted the Mercury Cougar parked on the side of the road near Mill Creek. Walking along the bank of the creek, they continued their search. As they reached a point nearly half a mile from the bridge in Wickersham, the group came across a strange sight. There was a pile of debris by the side of the creek, one which seemed unnatural compared to the rest of the surrounding area.

On closer inspection, it seemed as though the debris had been arranged – piled up in one place and then covered with a sheet of tarpaulin. Almost like a crown, an old tire had been thrown on top of the pile, holding everything in place. As the men got nearer, they could start to make out strange shapes. An army sleeping bag had been used for part of the cover. As they came closer, their worst fears began to materialize. Sticking out from the debris was a foot. The foot was still wearing a shoe.

At this point, nearly a full day from the time the two youngsters had set off together in the afternoon, Dan Oliver drove back down to the County Sheriff's Office. He was the bearer of bad news. As he told the police, they had discovered what was likely to be the bodies of Patrick and Susan. Not wanting to disturb the evidence, they had driven back out to the police. Learning of the discovery, the Sheriff took his men up to the creek to investigate further.

The police arrived to uncover the truth about what happened at the creek. They removed the tire and then the sleeping bag, taking away the debris. They found two bodies, those of Susan and Patrick. The bodies had been arranged, with Susan placed on top of Patrick. Her body was undressed, naked from the waist down, and with her green top jerked open to leave her breasts exposed. Patrick had been left clothed, still wearing the shirt and shorts he had on when the two set off the day before.

On closer inspection, they saw the two had been shot. The police could see the ravaged flesh around the entry wounds, the place where the bullets entered the bodies. For Susan, this was just below her left ear, a shot that would likely have killed her instantly. Patrick had more wounds. As well as having been shot through his arm, there was another entry wound in his shoulder. The coroner would later remark that this was likely a defensive maneuver, when the victim raised his hand in a desperate attempt to stop the bullet. The killer had fired anyway, and the bullet went straight through the man's arm and into his shoulder. This left Patrick open for a second shot, this one directly into his heart. The careful targeting of the shots seemed to indicate that the killer was skilled with his weapon.

It seemed as though – in both murders – the killer had intended to kill swiftly. When conducting an autopsy, it was discovered that Susan had not been the victim of any kind of sexual assault. There was a trace of a substance that had been spotted on the girl's body by one of the officers, but it was washed away by the staff in the funeral home before it could be tested. In many murders with female victims, signs of sexual assault can point the investigators towards a killer's motive. Without any such evidence, it made the deaths of Patrick and Susan a far more confusing and difficult problem to solve. Whereas most modern murders are approached with a wealth of forensic testing capabilities, the police in 1975 faced greater difficulties.

In a similar vein, the police found a few traces of fingerprints on the bodies. While the Sheriff's Office asked for assistance from better-equipped forces in having these analyzed, they were too slight to draw many conclusions. There were no matches on record, but if a suspect was put forward, then the lab might be able to match them against the evidence. Without a primary suspect, however, these prints were almost useless. The sheriff even sent the bullets to the FBI, hoping they would be able to conduct a ballistics report on the .357 caliber bullets. Again, the findings demonstrated that a conclusion could be drawn only if the local police were able to find a suspect with a .357 caliber handgun, on which the FBI could run tests designed to determine whether the firearm had shot these particular bullets.

So a lot of the investigator's efforts relied on good, old-fashioned police work. Calling for witnesses, asking for information, and chasing down leads. As it turned out, many people came forward to try to help. There were accounts from people who had heard gunshots, but these weren't especially useful accounts because they emerged from part of the area that was often used by firearm-enthusiasts for target practice.

One of the most important witnesses was a teenager named Diane Lackey. Diane had been in the area on the day in question and argued with her boyfriend. Storming off, she remembered hearing gunshots, and then coming across a man in a clearing in the woods. She estimated his age at somewhere in the late teens/early twenties. He was crouching down in the undergrowth, looking at something. He wasn't wearing a shirt. The description she gave was of a man of medium height, with brown hair and a slender build. As the two stared at one another, both suddenly seemed to become aware of the situation, and they both turned and ran. Diane fled back towards her boyfriend. If she saw the man again, she thought she might be able to recognize him.

There was one additional detail which seemed to be of importance. Diane believed the man might have been driving a small red car, one which she had seen in the area. It was a car that had also been spotted by other witnesses, though the owner had not been found. According to the reports, it was like a Ford Mustang, though no specific brand or model was given. Again, as with the bullets and the fingerprints, it was important information but didn't provide the police with enough to track down any specific individual.

The rest of the town wanted to help. In all, $5,000 was raised as a reward for any information which might lead to the murder of Patrick and Susan being solved. People were upset. They wanted answers. None were available.

The Sheriff's Office was dedicating a lot of time to the case. Between two of the best officers, over a thousand man-hours were poured into the investigation. This included contacting hundreds of people, taping over forty interviews, and compiling a series of transcriptions which added up to a nearly two-foot stack of paperwork. But despite the hours spent and the evidence gathered, there was little progress being made.

It's long been held that there are three components that make up a murder. These are the motive, the means, and the opportunity. To solve a murder, police attempt to figure out all three. The means, in this particular case, was the handgun. The opportunity was the fact that the picnic spot was so secluded. But that left the motive. Why, exactly, would someone want to murder these two youngsters, so beloved among the small Walla Walla community?

Identifying the motive was baffling the police department. They started considering more and more obscure explanations. One officer suggested that jealousy might have played a role, the killer stalking the pair out to the secluded site and murdering them in a pique of sexual frustration. Another suggested that Patrick's recent past in Europe had gotten him embroiled in an underground drugs ring, leading to the gang sending an assassin to dispatch the American, which would explain the professional marksmanship of the killer. Some people thought it might simply have been a deranged individual, a person with no motive beyond violence itself.

Trying to figure out the motive led to a lot of police time being spent chasing down dead ends. On the idea that the murders might have an international bent, one of the local officers spent a huge amount of time colluding with Interpol and the Mexican authorities, channels of investigation which ultimately led nowhere.

Months passed, and then years, and the authorities were no closer to discovering who had pulled the trigger on that fateful summer's day. People seemed reluctant to accept the possibility that the murders might have been the random actions of a solitary madman. The case remained unsolved. Like many of the unsolved murders in America, it became what is known as a cold case. Any hope that the killer of Patrick Oliver and Susan Savage might be brought to justice began to evaporate.

But, back in the summer of 1975, in the weeks following the murders, there was one man who went unnoticed. Resigning from his position as a jail guard after only six months, Robert Lee Yates began to pack his possessions into his red Dodge Dart, among them a .357 caliber Ruger handgun. The gun was part of one of his most beloved pastimes. He was a keen marksman and often entertained thoughts about joining the Army. For now, however, he was packing up and moving on. Leaving behind Walla Walla and the Wickersham Bridge (one of his favorite spots for target practice), Robert Yates also left behind the town, the people, and the unsolved murder. Later, his name would be on everyone's lips. In 1975, hardly anyone knew who he was.

In the Beginning

Robert Lee Yates had a history of violence in his family. Indeed, back in Oak Harbor, where Yates was born and raised, it's his father who goes by the name Robert. In that town, they know our killer simply as Bobby. Family casts a long shadow over the life we're about to explore. As far back as we can find, there have always been traces of violence.

In fact, as far back as 1945, murder was a familiar subject for the family. In 1945, Bobby Yates's grandmother took up a large double-sided axe and cut down her husband. The attack took place with Robert (Bobby's father) in the house. He could remember hearing the attack from his bed and went downstairs to investigate. There, he found his father dying on the floor in the kitchen. In the other room, his mother was sitting comfortably in a chair. It was a surreal scene.

The woman had been through a great deal. She had eleven children, and her husband was often away from the home, working a job which meant that he was rarely on the scene to play the pivotal role of the father figure. Who knows what went on between them, but eventually, it simply became too much. The woman snapped, on an otherwise insignificant night. For the next seven years, she would be locked away in a mental health institution, trying to recover.

It's impossible that such a traumatic event would not have left an imprint on a child. In turn, Robert Yates senior no doubt passed on the aftereffects of the murder to his son. Perhaps unwittingly, but there are few things which will shape a person more than witnessing one parent's murder by another. Still, the father tried his best to raise his son right.

Robert Lee Yates – Bobby to most – was remembered by many as a quiet kid. He wasn't the trouble-making type, seemingly a well-behaved, well-mannered, and well-meaning boy who hardly stood out among his generation. The good reputation of the town of Oak Harbor surely added to this. Whereas some murderers will look back on their destitute upbringing in crowded inner-cities, Bobby Yates was raised in a good, safe community.

The town was located on Whidbey Island, one of the most scenic and popular parts of northwestern America. Here, one could enjoy stunning views of the Pacific Ocean one moment and then turn to see the breathtaking backdrop of the Olympic Mountains the very next. Between, there were rivers, forests, creeks, and endless natural beauty. For a young kid growing up, this meant the chance to fish, shoot, hike, camp, and ride dirt bikes at any moment. It's hard to imagine anywhere in the United States better suited to raising an energetic, outdoorsy young boy.

Robert senior was a religious man. Perhaps understandably, given what he had seen in his life, he was heavily involved in the Seventh-day Adventist Church. It wasn't a big congregation, typically topping out at around a hundred people. The denomination differs from mainstream Protestantism. Not only do they observe Saturday as the Sabbath (rather than Sunday) but they believe in the imminent return to Earth of Jesus Christ. Robert brought his young son into the fold, preaching to him the values held by the Church.

It was a close bond between father and son. The two were known to share everything. Everything, except for a secret. Allegedly, the only piece of information Bobby kept from his father related to one of the family's neighbors. When Bobby was just six years old, the neighbor (five years older than Bobby) was said to have sexually molested him. Like many victims of sexual abuse, Bobby told no one. Everything else, however, he shared with his father. It meant the two were incredibly close while Bobby was growing up.

One of their favorite activities was baseball. There was a Little League team in the town, with Robert as the coach. On the team, Bobby learned how to pitch well enough that he'd go on to play for the Oak Harbor Wildcats in later life. Even to his teammates, Bobby didn't stand out. They didn't remember him as being particularly shy or particularly outgoing. Not venturing too far towards any social extreme, Bobby was pretty much a typical kid. A bit quiet, maybe, but not so much that it was notable. To many people, he was easy enough to forget about.

Like many a growing boy, Bobby took on chores around the neighborhood to earn a bit of pocket money. Over time, he worked mowing lawns, pumping gas, even harvesting peas. Typically these jobs paid a couple of dollars an hour. It wasn't much, but it was enough for a small town boy to entertain himself. That included, for a while, a steady girlfriend. She moved away before the end of Bobby's senior year in high school, however, so he skipped the homecoming dance. Instead, he stayed at home and played games with one of his closer friends, Al Gatti.

Gatti remembers Bobby Yates well, and the rest of the family. It was a respectful family, he recalls, and Bobby was much loved. In his opinion, anyone would be happy to have had the Yates family as their neighbors. Al and Bobby broke from one another after high school. While the former joined the army, the latter decided to go to college. Bobby attended the Skagit Valley College starting in 1970 and came out in the spring of 1972 with a degree in General Studies.

Despite going off to college during the tail end of the 1960s/early 1970s, Bobby Yates refrained from engaging in many of the social activities of the day. He didn't smoke or drink and, while many young men were growing their hair long, Bobby's hair stayed short. Rather than joining in with the more rebellious members of his generation, Bobby was happy with his hunting, shooting, and hiking.

Bobby Yates loved being outdoors. It wasn't uncommon for him and Gatti to spend days on end hiking through the mountains to their favorite fishing spots and then sitting for hours, catching trout.

Family life was something of a sudden change. After graduating from college, Bobby had returned to Walla Walla and pretty much picked up where he had left off. Though it wasn't mentioned much, Bobby had already been married once. In something of a whirlwind romance, he had married a woman named Shirley Nylander when he was twenty years old. The couple seemed to fall in love quickly and, after the marriage, they were just as quick to move in together. They chose to move to College Place, where they could study at Walla Walla College. It was an important institution to Bobby, as it was run by the Seventh-day Adventists.

But the marriage was doomed to fail. After only eighteen months together, Shirley moved out of the house. She wanted a divorce and Bobby seemed all too happy to oblige her. By this point in time, he had already met someone else. There was another student at Walla Walla College, a girl named Linda Brewer. The attraction to her was more than enough to get over the crumbling of his first marriage and Bobby Yates found himself falling in love once again.

Indeed, it wasn't long before Bobby and Linda were married. It was a shorter time still before the marriage was annulled. Bobby hadn't waited long enough – the divorce from Shirley was still not final – and technically they were still married. The first ceremony might have been rendered moot, but it was harder to dispute the child which was born six months later. The couple's first child was born in 1974 and it left Bobby facing a difficult decision. He was at a crossroads in his life and needed to decide on what he was going to do next.

In need of a regular paycheck, Bobby took a position working for the local prison. As a corrections officer, he was able to stay in Walla Walla and work at the Washington State Penitentiary. It was 1975, and all seemed to be going well. And it did, for about six months. Then, without much warning, Bobby decided to quit. Working as a prison guard, it seemed, was not for him. He didn't offer much of an explanation to his family, so people were slightly confused as to why he would leave a decent enough job. Apparently, it was in order to pursue an alternative career, one which would get him out of the area. As it happened, the summer of 1975 in Walla Walla was beset by the news of the murder of Patrick Oliver and Susan Savage. Nobody thought to investigate the former prison guard who was suddenly moving out of the area to join the military.

For years, Bobby had been enthralled with the idea of flying. As someone who spent a great deal of time in the countryside, he had no doubt seen the eagles and other birds soaring above the mountains. He longed to take to the air himself. For most Americans, however, such a dream was drastically out of their reach. Learning to fly was an expensive hobby. There was only one way a working class American like Bobby Yates could take to the air. He joined the Armed Forces.

Joining the military accomplished two things. Firstly, it allowed Bobby to indulge his aviation fantasies. Secondly, it was a steady paycheck. As a new father, he needed to be sure of a decent income to keep his wife and child clothed and fed. Thankfully, Bobby managed to pass the tests and did well enough to become a full-fledged pilot. But as Linda was spending more and more time with her new husband, she was starting to notice that he had strange tendencies.

One of the first incidents came around a month after the wedding. Linda, now living with Bobby, discovered that her husband had drilled a hole in the wall. The hole allowed him to see through to the neighbor's bedroom, meaning he could watch the couple have sex without them knowing. Linda was disgusted. She packed her bags and left. Eventually, however, she would return to her husband. It would be the start of a series of volatile reactions, periods in which Linda would desert Bobby, disgusted by one thing or another. She would pack up, gather the kids, and leave Bobby behind. But, usually, they reconciled.

A similar incident took place in the middle of the 1980s. While Bobby was stationed in Alabama, living there with his family, Linda grew tired of the constant arguments and fighting with her husband. Taking the kids, she moved back to Walla Walla. But the little girls loved their father. Every day they pleaded with their mother to make up with their father. Part of the reason was love, in that they wanted their family to be complete, but part of it was financial. Without Bobby's military pay, Linda and the girls were poor. It was hard to survive for long without money and the family's standard of living plummeted whenever Linda left Bobby. Part of the reason for their near-inevitable reconciliations was the security offered by Bobby's regular income. It would become a theme throughout the marriage.

When most kids dream of flying, they imagine themselves as airplane pilots. Bobby's career path was slightly different, however. His real skill lay in piloting helicopters. Slower than the fighter jets and bomber planes, the helicopters demanded a different approach. Their function was often much closer to the ground, closer to the action. Flying a helicopter in the American military was an incredibly demanding job but Bobby Yates was very good at it.

He was such a good pilot that, during the eighteen years he flew in the military, Bobby received many medals. All of them denoted some noteworthy, heroic, or accomplished act. Not only did Bobby spend time stationed in Germany during the Cold War, but he was one of the chopper pilots who flew in Operation Desert Storm, the United States' first invasion of Iraq. But there were also humanitarian missions. After Hurricane Andrew devastated large swathes of Florida in 1992 – at the time, the most destructive hurricane in American history – Bobby was part of the relief effort. His helicopter passed over the city, shipping food in, and shipping people out.

Among those who knew him in the military, Bobby was something of a complicated character. His skill was never in doubt. People often commented on the bravery demonstrated by the pilot and how adept Yates was as maneuvering the helicopter in even the most difficult of circumstances. They described him as safety conscious. When he was part of the peacekeeping force dispatched to Somalia, these skills were in high demand. But the posting also revealed the darker side of Bobby's character. While stationed in the African country, eating nothing but army rations for a month, Bobby decided that he and his friends should have a barbecue. While flying in the helicopter, he took it upon himself to shoot a wild pig. It broke dozens of military regulations and very nearly resulted in Bobby being court martialed. Even though no one got hurt, people were furious. After the anger died down, people turned the incident into something of a joke. But it demonstrated Bobby's often lax regard for the rules, especially when it came to killing.

In all, Yates's time in the military was a success. While Linda spent her time raising the kids, Bobby was racking up almost two decades worth of valued service. It seemed, however, that he was happy to keep the military and the domestic aspects of his life completely separate. Linda, remembering when she would be invited to gatherings, could see the strangeness in the overlap between the two worlds. When she talked to Bobby's colleagues, they occasionally seemed unaware that Bobby even had a wife.

In 1995, when Bobby transferred to Alabama, this became more acutely felt. Bobby was no longer touring the dangerous parts of the globe and providing air support. His expertise now meant that he was educating the next generation of helicopter pilots. Stationed in Fort Rucker, he had to go through a period of training himself, spending seven hours a day perfecting his knowledge so he could become one of the country's best instructors.

Linda and Bobby would sometimes go to parties being held on the base, and it was here Linda was able to see the other side of Bobby, the one which his military friends knew. When he was having a few drinks, she would watch as her husband mooned and flirted with other women. He gave his name as James Bond, lying to anyone he met. It came as quite a shock to Linda. But, with the military pay still being essential, she tolerated Bobby's behavior.

Things came to an abrupt halt, however. Only eighteen months from being eligible for the full military pension and a completed career, Bobby shocked everyone by handing in a request to leave. There was no explanation, no details given as to why he might want out of the Armed Forces after spending so long in the one career. It confused some people, annoyed others. Some were just left bemused. Taking a bonus for putting in for early resignation (though only a fraction of the benefits package due to those who completed their careers) Bobby Yates packed up the family and moved from Alabama to Spokane.

It might not have been that crazy a move. At the time, the military was replacing the helicopters Bobby knew so well, effectively making his role redundant. With the politicians reducing the numbers in the Armed Forces, there were benefits available to those who voluntarily left. For Bobby, this meant keeping a portion of his annual wage (roughly $20,000), and that he was free to do as he pleased. Having spent over twenty-one years in the military, some speculated that Bobby was simply bored.

But there might have been an even more pressing issue encouraging Bobby Yates to drop everything and move away from Alabama. In 1995, on the 9th of August, the authorities discovered the body of Tarayon Corbitt. Corbitt was a prostitute, a man who would often dress in women's clothing. He was found wearing a woman's outfit, dumped on the side of a road near Fort Rucker. The killer had used a .45 caliber handgun to shoot Corbitt twice in the face. As soon as the local police came across the body and realized it was a homicide, their attentions naturally turned towards the massive military base located nearby.

Bobby Yates was definitely in the area at the time and, as the authorities later noted, he certainly knew the place well. Even though he traveled all across the country attending and teaching at flight schools, Bobby was in Fort Rucker on the 18th of August, 1995, having graduated from a course that he had been attending. Just over a week later, Yates received an award to mark fifteen years of service as a helicopter pilot, proving he was definitely in the area at the time of the murder, though he wasn't around for long.

But the authorities never accused Bobby Yates of the murder of Tarayon Corbitt. After Yates left the area, and the state as well, the local police's jurisdiction was whittled down to almost nothing. Detectives who worked on the case, however, have described their belief that – having carried out the murder of the prostitute – Yates panicked and fled the scene. It would certainly tally with some of the events which we will cover later in this book, as well as the mysterious murders discussed in the prologue. So the theory goes, Bobby Yates was all too happy to resign from the military if it meant that he could escape the possible close scrutiny of the police.

Instead, Bobby and his family moved to Washington. It would be in Spokane that Yates would carry out the crimes that led to his eventual sentence of 407 years. However, aside from those convictions, there was a string of murders in which Yates was suspected, or has since been accused of being involved in. The deaths of Melinda Mercer and Connie Lafontaine Ellis in Tacoma led to an accusation but not a conviction. In both cases, the body was dumped in a remote spot and both murders occurred when Yates happened to be in the area. But, as was the case in Alabama, Yates seemed to slip by unnoticed at the time. It was only later that people made the connections.

In 1996, Yates had made his departure from the military and moved to Spokane. The family came too. Spokane was a small city, with just under 200,000 people. It was enough to allow for a community feeling without the necessity of knowing every single person you met. As big as Washington State is, the city was around 150 miles from Bobby Yates's home town of Walla Walla. Moving back to the area, Linda had hoped, might rekindle the love in the marriage. But it was not to be.

By this time, there seemed to be an awareness – for Linda, at least – that the love had dissipated from the relationship. She could tell Bobby no longer loved her like he once had done and, in truth, she felt the same way. But there was a reason to stay together – the kids. They loved their father and Linda did not want to be the one who broke up the family unit. She persevered with the relationship, suffering in silence as she lived out the reality of a loveless marriage.

At first, Bobby had hoped he might be able to put his piloting skills to good use. He still had a reduced wage coming in from the military's severance package but it wasn't enough. He needed a job and the natural inclination was to take on something that involved helicopters. Only, there weren't many calls for a chopper pilot in civilian life. Instead, Bobby took a position working in a factory that assembled the electronic instruments used in heavy machinery. One of the bosses at the company, Pantrol Inc., remembered Bobby staying with them up until 1997, and that he was a quiet worker who seemed fairly average and friendly enough. It was the same story that had followed Yates around for years. Friendly enough, but not too noticeable or memorable.

Bobby ran into a problem when Pantrol's business slowed down, and he needed to find another position. He went to work at the nearby aluminum processing plant. There, he was remembered in a similar fashion. By this point, he was slightly older and, for his younger co-workers, he became something of a father figure. Present, dependable, approachable. Hardly the traits you'd attribute to a serial killer.

Military life might have been difficult to leave behind, however. In 1997, Bobby Yates applied for a position in the Washington National Guard. It might not be the Army, but it was as close as he could get out in Washington. At any rate, he was far more qualified than most of the recruits. Bobby spent three years with the National Guard, but a medical examination soon found an issue and issued a decree that meant he was grounded, forbidden from flying helicopters. For almost a year, Robert Lee Yates Junior was forbidden from taking to the skies. As it happened, this period lasted from the spring of 1997 to the spring of 1998. During that time, people began to die.

This was the time when Bobby Yates's true nature rose to the surface. Locked in a loveless marriage, forbidden from flying his helicopters, having abandoned his sizeable military pension, Yates took on a new hobby. While there would be rumors and suspicions that became apparent later on, it was during this period that Yates truly unleashed his fury on the population of Spokane.

But Bobby was clever, or at least, he thought he was. He chose to target those people whom he believed society would not miss. The majority of his targets would be prostitutes, women who existed on the fringes of society. It would be harder to notice if they were missing, and less likely the courts would trust any peer witnesses, should something go wrong. They operated in the shadows, away from the mainstream of society. Furthermore, as long as it was 'only' prostitutes that he was killing, the people in Spokane seemed to pay the murders little attention. Unlike the deaths of Patrick Oliver and Susan Savage, there was no community outrage, no massive reward offered, and no concerted effort to catch the criminal behind the murder. Often, the deaths went without comment.

Over the course of the next year, as we will see in the coming chapters, Robert Yates unleashed a campaign of brutality against the women in the area. He would spend the time learning about which targets he should focus on, how best to avoid detection, how to cover his tracks, and how to get the most satisfaction from the hideous acts he was set on carrying out. Often, he would hang out in truck stops and diners, often with crowds of the prostitutes he would end up targeting. Moving under an assumed name, he would educate himself about their habits, meaning he was fully prepared to murder when the time was right. During this time, he would use drugs, often with the women who would end up as his victims. Some would describe him as emotionless and calculating, while others would say he something of a romantic. To his family at home, the very idea that Bobby Yates might be killing prostitutes was bizarre. When he was eventually arrested, everyone from family members to prostitutes who had known Bobby was shocked.

One thing is for sure, those who ended up dead on the side of the road misunderstood the true nature of Bobby Yates. In the end, that would be what killed them.

Finding a Body

The date was the 26th of August, 1997. Since it was a warm day in Washington, many people decided to take advantage of the state's scenery and stroll around town. One such man was Larry Jones, a former Army man who had served in Vietnam. These days, he often searched for empty soda cans while he walked, hoping to turn them over to the recycling plant for a bit of extra cash. It was 11:00 in the morning as he walked down East Springfield Street. There, he found a body, half-hidden beneath a tree.

As it happened, the corpse was placed in the long grass next to a couple of metal tins. The tins themselves might have attracted Jones at first, but the body caught his attention like a tractor beam. It was half naked; a woman. She had been there a while, the skin showing signs of having been exposed to the weather. When the detectives surveyed the area, they would find a gallon of blood splattered across a nearby parking lot. The body had been dragged from the lot, across an embankment, and then hidden beneath the tree with the other garbage. At this point, there was no telling how long it had been there. The rot had already started to set in, and decomposition was taking hold. It was even tough to tell the gender of the deceased, though there was a strong suspicion that this was a woman. Nationality, profession, identity – all of these were almost impossible to determine at first glance. The police were called. They were about to have a busy day.

That same day, just a few hours later, a storm arrived. For the alfalfa farmers in the area, this meant a desperate attempt to finish the harvest before the weather affected the crops. Out on a farm near Mount Spokane, one family set about gathering quickly, worried looks shooting over to the horizon. The storm was darkening in the distance.

It was around 5:00 in the afternoon. As the alfalfa piled up on the back of the tractor trailer, the fetid stench of death began to rise up from the field. Kevin Kailin, the owner of the farm, followed his nose. It might have been an animal, alone and rotting in the field. The smell seemed to be emanating from the tall grass, close to the base of a tree. The trunk was fitted with a big No Trespassing sign. As the rest of the family finished bringing the harvest in, Kevin put in a call to the Sheriff's Office. Before long, they had to call in the homicide squad as well.

Again, the body had been dumped just off the side of a road. Whereas the parking lot victim had been dragged over an embankment, this corpse seemed to have been dragged out into a field. Strangely enough, it was an open area. Apart from the tree with the warning sign and the occasional dense patch of brush and hedgerow, the eye could see far out across the field. Once again, the rot seemed to have destroyed any opportunity to make an immediate identification.

It would have been impossible to forget the sight of the corpse. While the family who owned the farm were told to keep their distance, the police had no such luck. Already infected with maggots, the corpse was coated in leather-like skin, rotted to the point where trying to determine a race by hue alone was a real problem. Filling out the paperwork, looking at the bone structure and the features, the police guessed that the woman was likely either Asian, Indian, or African American. It was difficult to narrow it down any further.

The body had been dumped in such a way that it was facing up towards the heavens. The arms had collapsed up and around the head, with the legs sticking straight out and downwards. Seen from above, the body could be likened to the images of men and women which decorated the sides of Grecian pottery, laid out flat. It definitely did not seem as though this was a deliberate arrangement, more that the killer had simply deposited the woman on the ground and stopped caring almost immediately after. No grave had been dug, and only a cursory attempt had been made to conceal the corpse from prying eyes. Fortunately for the murderer, the surrounding grass and vegetation had softened under the weight of the body, so it sank down and out of sight. It was a corner of the field few people ever went to. It was only when you got within about fifteen feet of the site that you could actually see a body at all. It was the smell that caught their attention, and that was only a result of the decomposition. Another few weeks, and it might have gone unnoticed.

The detectives attempted to piece together what information they could. The clothes were still on the victim, and included a blouse with long sleeves which could just as easily have been a dress. It had been unzipped, pulled up past the shoulders and over the victim's black bra. That too had been tugged at, pulled up almost over the head and neck, leaving the body essentially naked from the chest downwards.

It was summer, so the light was lasting. Despite only discovering the body in the early evening, the detectives could begin to piece together some of the events that had led to the woman's body being dumped. To the east, heading back towards the road, they could see the grass had been marked and the brush bent and moved. This seemed to indicate something heavy had been dragged through, creating a path from the road to the dumping site. Looking closely at the clothing, it seemed to offer confirmation that the body had been dragged, with dirt and grass stains showing that the killer had grabbed the victim by the ankles and tugged her along. At some point along the way, he switched position and started dragging the body head first.

The police began to photograph the entire area. As the sun set and the light faded, it was becoming more and more difficult to assess the scene of the crime. They would have to suspend their process until the morning, arriving back with the light. Leaving a patrolman to watch over the scene, not wanting anyone to shift so much as a twig, the detectives departed for the night at around 9:30. Within twelve hours, they were back again.

The body stayed behind. Moving the body is one of the last things to happen on a crime scene. There are just too many clues hidden on and around the victim's corpse to warrant less than extreme caution. In crimes such as this, violent attacks with a seemingly sexual motive and an unknown assailant, getting together a profile of the attacker is essential. By preserving the scene as best they could and dedicating as much time as possible to studying the body *in situ*, the detectives hoped to increase their chances of understanding exactly what had happened.

The examination of the crime scene went on for days. During this time, the police checked every inch of the surrounding field in the hope that it might turn up some tiny clue here or there. They began to find bits and pieces. One of the most significant clues was a condom found near the road. Next to this were a pair of high heeled shoes – black and in the victim's size – and some underwear, as well as the broken antenna from a car radio. Following the trail back to the location of the body, they found the occasional blood stain, which they collected and sent for testing. On cutting away at the brush surrounding the body, they also discovered a pair of black underpants (in a small size) and a towel that was covered in blood.

Furthermore, close examination of the body was starting to add to the potential identity of the victim. She had long, dark hair, but it had been so matted with dirt and blood that trying to tell the exact color was almost impossible. Similarly, her build seemed to be slight, but the extent of the decomposition made checking such a fact very difficult indeed. Jewelry was found, including two small earrings and two rings on her fingers. One of these rings was a simple gold band on her right ring finger, inlaid with a single pearl, and a smaller green stone on either side. The victim had painted her toenails and fingernails in the same purple color and seemed to have used glitter on the toenails as well. While it was impossible imagine what she looked like from the corpse's rotten face, these details might help a friend or relative identify the body.

In the same vein, the amount of decomposition made it tough to figure out the exact cause of death. The body had been rotting for so long that any possible trauma wounds were now part of a complicated quilted network of discoloration. Indeed, significant chunks of flesh seemed to be completely missing from the body. It was unclear whether these were lost, destroyed, or had been taken by animals. The clothes gave a better hint, where the shoulder of the blouse demonstrated a defect that correlated with a small circular perforation in the body. It was potentially the sign of a bullet wound.

At the time, detectives struggled to link together the body found in the alfalfa fields with the one found near the parking lot. (It would have been impossible to link the murders to those in Walla Walla some twenty years previous.) Murders in Spokane were not common. Within a week, details on the two bodies had been published in all the major local papers. The police department was suddenly under a great deal of pressure to solve these murders.

One of the first steps was to find out as much as possible about the bodies. After the crime scenes had been investigated down to every last detail, the authorities brought the corpses in to conduct autopsies. Here, they began to notice even smaller details, adding to the larger picture.

For the woman who had been found in the alfalfa field, the doctor conducting the autopsy pointed out that a button was missing from the left cuff of the victim's shirt. Also, the victim appeared to be missing her fake eyelashes from one eye. The autopsy confirmed the cause of death – a gunshot wound to the chest and the shoulder – and suggested that the weapon used had been a .22 caliber pistol.

The body in the parking lot died from similar wounds. This time, the killer had used a .25 caliber handgun and the victim had been shot in the head. Less badly decomposed, the police were able to carry out fingerprint checks on this woman, and discovered a match. Heather Hernandez had been twenty years old, originally hailing from Arizona, and was a known drifter. Because of this, few people knew much about her. Heather was something of a mystery and had not been in Spokane for very long at all.

Finding out the identity of the woman in the field was more difficult. After asking around and conducting the autopsy, the police came up with a name: Jennifer Kim. It was likely not her real name, but it was the name she gave to many people. Jennifer worked as a prostitute and was, they learned, just nineteen years old. She and Heather knew each other – even if they were not directly associated – and often moved in overlapping social circles. Furthermore, on digging a little deeper, the police confirmed that Jennifer Kim was an alias. The girl's real name was Jennifer Joseph.

This meant there were difficult phone calls to be made. Now armed with the victims' identities, the police had to get in touch with the families and let them know what had happened. In doing so, they made another discovery about Jennifer. According to her parents, she was not only lying about her name, but her age as well. In fact, she was just sixteen years old.

As the police were able to learn more about the two victims, the pictures became clearer. Jennifer, they learned, was the daughter of a career army man and had traveled all around the country in her youth. With her mother now in Hawaii, she was supposedly in town with her boyfriend. However, he had moved on some weeks before and left Jennifer behind. The police made an effort to get in touch with him. He could well be a suspect.

The investigations were tough. Part of any such process involves meeting and talking to the victims' friends and family, moving through their social circles in order to try and build up a more complete picture of their lives. However, as both women were prostitutes, this was tough. Police know sex workers do not move in conventional social circles. Often operating outside of the law, those in their social groups can be unwilling to talk openly with police officers. They might be fellow prostitutes, their customers, drug dealers, or others who operate at the fringes of society. Trying to get information in these circumstances can be difficult and it can act as an additional layer of security for the killer.

For Robert Yates, this meant being able to evade the police with ease. Over the course of many years, he had picked up a habit of socializing in the seedier parts of town. Spending time away from his wife – sometimes pretending he was at work – he would have no compunction about wasting away hours in truck stops or bars, the parts of E. Sprague Avenue in Spokane that were sometimes referred to as Skid Row. If, as it seemed likely, he killed the two youngsters back in Walla Walla and the prostitute near the military base in Alabama, he was now turning his attentions towards those whose disappearance would not be noticed.

These two murders are often regarded as the starting point of Robert Lee Yates junior's killing spree. Over the course of the next eighteen months, he would spend more and more time around prostitutes and more bodies would begin to pile up across Spokane. As is the case when a police department is investigating murders, it seemed at first that these two deaths were separate, individual tragedies. They had no idea of what Yates was capable of doing. Yates seemed to have spent decades watching and observing, learning how best he could act out his sadistic fantastic without running the risk of being caught. With the murders of Jennifer Joseph and Heather Hernandez, he demonstrated the first real examples of his new approach to murder.

Yates's 1979 Ford van would become a more and more familiar sight throughout the rougher parts of the city. Providing people with a fake name, Yates would get to know potential victims. This meant he was no stranger to having sex with prostitutes. Indeed, many sex workers knew him by his (false) name and almost seemed to trust him. He paid, he wasn't violent, and he seemed happy to enjoy the occasional drink, the occasional joke, and the occasional dalliance with drugs. To them, he was a regular customer. Little did they know that Yates was beginning to target his new acquaintances.

But, in telling this story, there is something of a problem. Bobby Yates has refused to discuss his murders in detail, so putting together the story of this serial killer is often a case of seeing the world through the eyes of the police force. While we might wish we could understand exactly what Yates was thinking as he drove out to rural spots to dump the latest body, his true thoughts and emotions remain as much a mystery today as they were at the time of his capture. If we want to understand this serial killer, we must follow in the footsteps of the men who caught him. As the officers delved deeper and deeper into the Spokane underworld, they found out just how hard it can be to investigate in a community who resented their very presence. Along the way, Yates always seemed to be one step ahead. In the next chapter, we will start to look much more closely at the investigation and how it grew over the course of time.

An Investigation

The detectives – led by two men named Ruetsch and Grabenstein – attempted to track down girls who might have worked with the victims in the past. Of all the people who socialized with sex workers in Spokane, it was the girls' colleagues who seemed most likely to talk to the police. While they might not have appreciated the cops' constant efforts to chase them from the streets, if there was a killer focusing on prostitutes, then it was in their interests to help keep him off the streets.

One of the stories they heard concerned Jennifer Joseph and time she spent on the corner of Sprague and Thor. The witness described how Jennifer, on the evening of the 16th of August, got into a car with a man aged roughly thirty to forty years old. It was a sports car, she said, likely a Porsche. Together with the detectives, the witness agreed to drive downtown and point out the exact spot where Jennifer usually worked; the place where she could be found most nights.

In truth, many of Jennifer Joseph's colleagues didn't like her. The reason was that Jennifer was part Korean, a racial mix which seemed to play well with the clients. While most girls were bored, strolling up and down the street, Jennifer would hardly have to wait any time at all between the so-called 'dates.' As soon as one person dropped her off, another picked her up. Jennifer could have been making hundreds of dollars every night, something many of the other girls resented.

One of the first places the detectives took their witness was a used car lot. They had been told that the man who picked up Jennifer was driving a Porsche but they wanted to make sure. After they showed the girl an actual Porsche, she excitedly pointed at another car, claiming that it was just like the one she had told them about. It was a Chevy Corvette, a coupe from 1975. It wasn't even in the car lot, it was parked on the street. Either way, the girl was convinced that this was the exact vehicle. Her testimony might not have filled the detectives with confidence, but it was progress all the same.

Knowing the car makes of Jennifer's and Heather's customers was important. Among the other sex workers who walked along the Spokane streets, customers were better known by their vehicles than their faces or names. At night, with many men reluctant to identify themselves, it was easier to tell apart the clients by the cars they drove. For regular clients, this was even more important. When talking to one another, the girls might discuss a red Ford pickup truck or a black Mercedes. In a world where most people were already lying about their identities – both the prostitutes and clients – few people could lie about the cars they drove. Find the right car, and the detectives might be able to find the killer.

The white Corvette was the last car anyone could remember Jennifer getting into. It didn't necessarily mean the man driving this particular car was the killer, but it was the best lead the detectives had at this point. Due to the nature of the work in question, such a meeting could have lasted five minutes or two hours. Because Jennifer was in such high demand among the clients, it only increased the likelihood that she was in and out of the Corvette in a short span of time. Whoever had been the last person to pick her up seemed to be the likeliest suspect, the man who had put the gun to her head and pulled the trigger. The same was true in the death of Heather Hernandez.

Due to the locations where the bodies were found – Heather inside the city limits and Jennifer out in the country – the investigations were being handled by two different teams.

Investigating a murder is never like the movies. When you sit down in front of a film, you can be fairly certain that – give or take a few minutes – everything will be wrapped up in about two hours. The detours, dead ends, and red herrings are cut out for the sake of streamlining the process. But in real life, the vast majority of the work leads to nothing. This can be disheartening, soul-crushing work, and it is mostly a case of eliminating potential suspects rather than focusing in on a few key people. One of the people they wanted to talk to went by the name Roberts. It was thought this was almost definitely a fake name. The man supposedly shared an apartment with Jennifer and drove a brown Cadillac. Police had gone to the apartment to check but had been told that he was behind in the rent and had not been seen in a while. When Roberts returned, the detectives said, the manager of the apartment complex was to give them a call. While he might not be a key suspect, this Roberts was certainly worth some measure of the police's attention. When he came back to the complex, the detectives received a call. One of the most pressing matters that needed to be checked was the car itself. What was the condition of the Cadillac's aerial? If it was broken, it might tie the car to the spot where the body was found.

When the police were finally able to meet Roberts, they were intrigued. The man they met was not Robert Yates, whom they had no idea existed, but was instead a man who was a support worker for the sex industry. It was Roberts's job to act as a liaison between prostitutes and their clients, as well as preventing people from harassing and bothering the girls. Roberts, he admitted, was a false name, designed to make renting an apartment easier. Eventually, the real Roberts – who lived in Idaho – would find himself being chased by debt collectors who wanted money for a cell phone bill and unpaid rent, all racked up by the mysterious man.

But these unpaid bills and identity theft were minor issues when compared to the on-going murder investigation. Roberts – at least, the man pretending to be Roberts – seemed to be distraught over the death of Jennifer Joseph. Therefore, he had no problem letting the police look over his car, nor with giving them a sample of his blood. He even willingly offered himself up to take part in a lie detector test. The man wanted the killer to be found and to be removed from the line of suspicion himself.

It was a few days later when Detective Rick Grabenstein's efforts in getting to know Jennifer's colleagues was starting to pay off. He received a phone call from another sex worker, who described a 1970s van with a distinctive paint job that had been seen in the area. According to the girl, the van was a Chevy, mostly dark brown but with a lighter beige panel highlighted with brown flames along the side. On the back of the van was an eagle, right over the back door where one might normally expect to find the spare tire. The girl said the driver was white, was probably middle aged, and likely had brown hair. It was a pretty vague description, matching up to the biggest demographics in the city, but it was something. Grabenstein took down the information and asked to meet the girl in person. Reluctantly, she agreed.

Like many of the girls working in the sex industry, the witness's parents had no idea she was embroiled in prostitution. Never, she pleaded, contact her parents. That was the condition she gave when agreeing to talk to the police. Grabenstein agreed.

The first question asked by the detective was just what made the girl suspicious of this particular van. She must see hundreds of vehicles every day, what made this one stand out? It was a distinctive van, the girl replied, one which she had seen before that summer. Only, the first time she saw it, the windows were normal. Now they were tinted. Something in the girl's intuition told her this was suspicious. When the van had pulled up near her once, perhaps expecting her to stroll across to the open window, the girl had refused, claiming the van gave her "bad vibes." When she talked to another prostitute about the van, she had said that the driver was harmless. But something about the van dissuaded her from getting in. It must not have been a feeling shared by Heather Hernandez. According to the witness, she had seen Heather getting into that very same van just a few days before the police found her body.

As the detectives would find out later, it was not the first time the van had been used in a homicide. The case of Shannon Zielinski's murder had recently gone cold. It had happened in the summer of 1996, and was also handled by Detective Grabenstein. Shannon's body had been found by a bus stop used by school children. Like the victims he was currently investigating, Grabenstein remembered the woman having a gunshot wound to the head.

Just like the two murders in August of 1997, the death of Shannon Zielinski had occurred during the summer. Unbeknownst to the detectives, Bobby Yates was living nearby with his wife and their daughter at around this time. Sasha Yates, now grown up, was working at Certified Security Systems. She handled the night shift and her father agreed to drive her to work. Linda still kept an eye on her husband's movements and activities. Even though he had dropped their daughter off at 11:00 that night, he took hours to return. By 2:30 in the morning, he was still not home.

With Linda growing weary in the early hours of the morning, she decided to lock up the house, even though her husband wasn't home. She went to sleep. At 6:30 the next morning, she was woken up by the sound of someone banging on the front door. It was Bobby. Linda ran down the stairs and opened the door.

Bobby Yates stumbled into the room. Straight away, he moved towards the place where the family kept all their cleaning supplies. Linda stood by watching as Bobby, without explaining, snatched up every product he could find and took them out to the van. Linda followed. As she stepped out of the house and into the morning light, she could see something was wrong with the van. It was covered, the interior filled with splatter marks and blood spills. There was a small pull-down cot in the back of the vehicle. It was almost dripping with blood.

Linda had questions. But before she could say anything too accusatory, Bobby gave her an explanation. He had been driving, he said, along Ray Street. There, a man had been walking his dog. Without warning, the dog had jumped out in front of the van and – Bobby explained – the poor thing had been badly hurt. Desperate, the men put the dog in the back of the van, on top of the cot, and tried to reach a vet in time. The dog had bled everywhere. Taking out the bedding and the cushions, Bobby destroyed them. They were too soaked in dog's blood, he told her. The interior of the 1988 Chevy van looked like something from a war zone, but Linda accepted her husband's story. A dead dog seemed a viable explanation. As long as she didn't have to clean out the van herself, then it would do. Besides, it was too early in the morning to get into an argument over a dead dog.

But Detective Grabenstein knew none of this. He had worked on Shannon's death but had never heard of Bobby Yates, the brown van, or the dead dog. He noted the uneasiness of the witness and the details about the vehicle. While it wasn't much, it was probably worth knowing. Right now, he had other people who should be interviewed. First and foremost on this list was Marlin, Jennifer's boyfriend.

One of the first things Marlin was adamant about was that he was not a pimp. Often, in the sex trade, Grabenstein knew that the lines between 'boyfriend' and 'pimp' were blurred. But, sitting in front of him, Marlin was insistent that this was not the case. The two had met at a party a few months before, and had gotten involved in a serious relationship, to the point where the boy had met the girl's father. They had moved to Spokane and started living in a hotel. Jennifer would leave the room every day at around 3:00 to start working and Marlin wouldn't see her for hours. He had no idea where she went in this time.

According to what he told the detectives, Marlin had last seen Jennifer on the 16th of August at around 3:00 in the afternoon. As per her usual routine, a cab picked her up from the motel and drove her wherever she pleased. On the day in question, she had been wearing black trousers, a grey blouse, and black shoes. Besides some details about how she had worn her hair, and the underwear she might have been wearing, Marlin couldn't remember much. That was the last time he had seen her, but not the last time he had heard from her. Around 9:00 in the evening, she had called the room and informed Marlin she would be home at close to midnight. She asked what he might be cooking for dinner, but other than that, the two didn't have much to discuss.

When Jennifer failed to come home that night, Marlin had panicked. He had started asking the other girls whether they'd seen her, hearing similar stories to Grabenstein concerning a white Porsche driven by a middle-aged white guy. Marlin ended up staying in Spokane for another three days. As well as looking for Jennifer, he called her father a couple of times, desperate for more information. No one had any. Assuming she had simply ditched him to spend time with someone else, Marlin packed up and moved back to Tacoma, Washington. It was not unheard of for Jennifer to disappear for a day or two at a time, so he held off filing a missing person's report. When packing, Marlin made sure to take all of Jennifer's possessions. If she did come looking for them, then he hoped to get some answers from her. When the news came through that she had been found dead, those same belongings became a constant reminder of his girlfriend's fate. He knew the police would come looking for him soon enough. Marlin gave most of the possessions over to the police and let them take samples of his blood, as well as letting them examine his car. In Grabenstein's opinion, the boy seemed devastated by the death. The detectives seemed content to put Marlin to the side, for now.

By the 15th of September, it had been nearly a month since the bodies had been found, and the police had made very little progress. The closest thing to a breakthrough came when they heard reports of a traffic incident involving a car matching one of the descriptions they garnered during their time on the streets. It was an unrelated issue, but the car – a Chevy Corvette – matched the profile and, to make things more interesting, the car contained two handguns with calibers of .25 and .22. These seemed to match the guns used in the murders. The guns were immediately sent to the ballistics lab. According to the woman who had been riding as the passenger, the guns belonged to her. She agreed to have the guns tested but said little else.

When examined closely, the car became even more interesting. Not only was the antenna broken and missing, but it had recently been repainted. Whoever had recolored the car had done a bad job, getting paint on the lights. Also, the cops who pulled over the car said there had been a blood-splattered bedspread on the backseat. It seemed like a major boon, a real breakthrough. But first, the detectives had to wait on the ballistics report. They took everyone's details and allowed them to leave.

It was a week before the results of the ballistics report came back. The detectives had carried on investigating in this time, including spending time tracking down the owner of a Chevy SUV that had been seen in the area. It had led to nothing. After seven days, things were made even worse when the ballistics report indicated a negative correlation. In all likelihood, these guns were not the same ones used in the murders. The police were almost back to square one, with their most promising lead wiped out in an instant.

Around this time, Robert Yates junior was going about his day-to-day life, trying to pretend nothing out of the ordinary had taken place. At the time in question, he was driving a white Corvette. On the 24th of September, when traveling in his sports car, Yates happened to see the flashing of police lights in his rearview mirror. Not panicking, he casually pulled to the side of the road. As it happened, the place he had chosen to stop was just a few blocks from the spot where Jennifer Joseph had last been seen alive.

The policeman who had pulled Yates to the side of the road was just a regular cop. Typically, Officer Turman worked the so-called 'prostitution zone' that was located near East Sprague. As one of the men more familiar with the area, the detectives working the homicide case had given him a list of the vehicles they had identified as being in some way interesting. A white Corvette had been on that list. When Yates had failed to correctly signal a lane switch, the cop had an excuse to pull him over and get a closer look. It would not be the last mistake made that evening.

The second mistake might seem minor, but it had big ramifications. When jotting down the details of the traffic stop, the cop incorrectly identified the car Yates had been driving. While it was a Chevy Corvette, Turman wrote down Cam, short for Camaro. He noted it was in excellent condition, and went so far as to record the name, date, and time in his report. After he completed the form and allowed Yates to go about his business, the cop paid little attention to what happened next.

The process was simple. At the end of the shift, he would hand over the paperwork to an analyst. From there, it would be forwarded to the relevant officers. At least, it would have been, had the slight error not appeared on the form. The homicide team hadn't put out a request for any white Camaros. They never received the report, and never heard about Robert Yates and his white Corvette.

In some cases, the police will put out a description of cars or people they wish to learn more about. It's hoped that the public will be able to come forward with any missing information. But Grabenstein was concerned that, if they tried such a move, the killer would just ditch his car and they'd be no better off. By this time, there was a suspicion that the same man might have murdered both women, but they had no idea who. The list of potential suspects was long and mostly related to the types of cars seen moving through the area.

To make matters worse, more women had disappeared. No bodies had been found, but a number of sex workers had not been seen in days. Among them were Darla Scott, Shawn Johnson, and Laurie Wason. People had reported them missing but nothing had been found. The detectives began to take an interest. All three of the women were known to be affiliated with prostitution in one way or another, or they were known drug users. The local health clinic – which had a special unit to combat the spread of HIV among the city's sex workers – was also something of an unofficial source of information on such matters. The woman who worked there, Lynn Everson, could provide information on many of the girls walking the streets. The police kept their ears peeled for any news about these girls.

The Next Wave

Despite the hard work of the detectives, the interest of the public had waned. Two dead prostitutes was news, but not for very long. By November, the news cycle had moved on. The issue was about to be thrust back onto the stage, however, on the morning of the 5th of November. As a man was out walking his dog, passing along Hangman Valley Road, he began to notice something. It was the same route he walked every single day and, on each of the last five days, his dog had been strangely attracted to a specific spot on the route. Unable to see exactly what the dog wanted, he pressed on and ignored it. That was, he ignored it up until the 5th of November. On that morning, he decided to take a closer look. When he found the body, he called the police.

As the police examined the scene, they made a number of discoveries. Most obvious, at first, was the fact that the killer had attempted to bury the body. Located around sixty feet from the roadway – not close enough to see from the road, but near enough for a dog to catch the scent – it had been dumped near a small creek that ran alongside the street. The head, an arm, and a leg were all visible, though the rest of the body had been buried. The arm was clothed in a blue, long-sleeved shirt, material similar to a scrap which was lying on the ground near the body.

Grabenstein and his team were notified. As they looked over the scene, they noticed that there was another partial grave, but it seemed half complete. For some reason, the killer had started to dig one grave, had changed his mind, and then moved on to the final site. Maybe it was more out of sight. Maybe the ground was easier to move there. It wasn't clear.

The body itself was laid out on its back. The legs seemed to be curled up to the chest, though it was hard to tell. Not only was the body partially buried, but it had been there long enough that decomposition was a real problem. It had started to rot, and animals had been taking bites out of the flesh. As the detectives saw it now, the entire right side of the victim's head had no flesh on the skull. If you looked closely, you could see the teeth marks from the predators as they bit away the skin. To the rear of the head, a round wound seemed to indicate that this person had also been shot.

The animals had not only taken bites out of the head. They had also chewed at the shoulder, leaving ripped and torn skin, muscle, and sinew in the space just above the left elbow. It was a similar case when looking at the right foot and ankle. Not wanting to move the body at first for fear of disturbing clues, the extent to which the body had been ravaged post-mortem left the detectives with little hope of finding anything useful.

Perhaps the only real identifying element was the clothing. Though most of it was buried, it was possible to make out parts of the pattern – a large Mickey Mouse character printed on the front. The material was soaked in blood and was ripped and torn in places which seemed concurrent with the attack.

Removing the body took a long time. In all, the police dug down around six feet. Though the grave was shallow, they sifted through the excavated earth and plant matter surrounding the body, in the hope of finding any kind of clue. Anything that might even resemble evidence was carefully removed, documented, and stored.

The excavation took almost all day. Above, the weather threatened; it looked like rain. Worried that this might disturb the ground and hinder the recovery of any clues, the police covered the spot with a nylon sheet and took the body back to the morgue, ready for the coroner to examine.

The autopsy was conducted the next day. According to the doctor, the body belonged to a white woman who weighed between 120 and 140 pounds. She was about five and a half feet tall and could have been anywhere between 20 and 30 years old. The extreme nature of the decomposition made it difficult to be more exact.

Establishing the cause of death was easier. There were two gunshot wounds, both to the head. The shots had been fired from the left, entering the skull and passing through the brain. According to the report, the bullet would likely have been .25 caliber or smaller, but it passed through the skull and exited the other side, so it was not available for examination. Additionally, the coroner took swabs of the victim's genitals, mouth, and anus in order to check for signs of sexual assault and other traces of DNA.

It took even longer to figure out the identity of the victim. Dental records came back on the 12th of November and confirmed that this was Darla Scott, one of the missing sex workers from Spokane. As before, the detectives decided to pay a visit to everyone who Darla might have known, desperate to put together any pieces of the puzzle they could.

What emerged was a typical story. Darla was a drug addict. She had little contact with her parents these days but did have significant other in her life: her daughter. The baby's father, when questioned, revealed that Darla had quit drugs while she was pregnant, knowing they were harmful to the baby. She had hoped the child would keep her away from a life on the streets. It hadn't been the case. Not long after the birth, she had lapsed back into her habit.

The last time Darla had called her baby's father was back in October. She was in a Kmart in East Sprague, waiting to pick up some drugs. Though he tried to convince her to come and see him, to leave the drugs behind, she couldn't. It was the last time he heard from her.

Darla, like many girls in East Sprague, balanced her work with her drug habit, and they often went hand in hand. Occasionally, she might kick the habit for a week or two, but never for very long. Sometimes, rather than staying around in Spokane, she would take to the road with one of her trucker friends. Typically smuggled aboard the big rigs without the truckers' employers knowing, girls like these would travel from state to state, having sex and occasionally doing drugs with the drivers. It was fairly common for the girls in the area to do this and one of the truckers who had recently spent time with Darla became known to the police.

Getting in contact with him was difficult, however, as he was out of town, probably working. Instead, the detectives first talked to his landlord. The trucker rented a room in Spokane and would occasionally return between shifts. It wasn't uncommon for Darla to return with him and the landlady knew her. It seemed that, when she was on the road in a truck, Darla found it easier to stay away from drugs. It was when she was stationary, staying in the city for any amount of time, that she turned back to narcotics. The landlady had seen the couple just after they returned from one job. Apparently, it was Darla's birthday the next day, and they were preparing a celebratory dinner. But before they could do that, Darla hooked up with one of her old friends. She slipped back into the drugs and the trucker was despondent. The way the landlady told it, he was heartbroken. Even if he loved her, it was becoming clear the only way Darla would escape the addiction was through death.

It was a similar story to the one the detectives heard from another acquaintance. Though he claimed to have been her boyfriend previously, he said he couldn't deal with her working as a prostitute. Rather than jealousy, he claimed that it was the inherent danger of the business that put him off. Darla refused to give it up. In the end, he was proved right.

The first person to report that Darla was missing was her twin sister, but at that stage, many people weren't concerned. They assumed she had simply relapsed or had taken to the road with another trucker. But rumors began to spread. Some people said she had gotten embroiled in a drugs bust and a local dealer had been murdered as a result. They thought she might be in jail.

Certainly, Darla Scott was known to the local police. She was an informer, and one of the best in the area. She knew a lot about what was happening on the streets and didn't mind telling the authorities. If anyone spotted her in the company of the police, she would pass the officers off as clients. It was a lie, but one people were willing to believe. When she was found murdered, people who knew she was informing wondered if her murder might have been an act of vengeance, a retribution for snitching.

Eventually, as the homicide detectives learned more and more about Darla, they realized the list of potential suspects was growing to a ridiculous length. If they had to consider everyone whom Darla had lied to, cheated, stolen from, snitched on, or just simply annoyed, the list would include half the criminal underworld in the city and a lot of regular folk as well. The further they dug into Darla's life, the more they discovered it was a ticking time bomb of tragedy.

While the detectives were busy attempting to uncover the truth about Darla Scott and trying to figure out whether it was connected to the other deaths, another tragedy was revealed. This time, on the 7th of December, the police found the body of

Melinda Mercer. She was found in Tacoma, a city far away from Spokane (though still in Washington) and it seemed, at first, as though it might be difficult to link the cases.

Melinda's body was found naked. It had been left out in the open, with little attempt to hide it. Nearby, the spent casing from a .25 caliber handgun was found. There was no purse, wallet, or money at the scene, and it seemed as though a car had been used to bring the body to this particular spot before it was unceremoniously thrown out. Once they identified her, the local police had the name Melinda Mercer to work with. They discovered she was a waitress, a well-regarded and good natured woman, who also happened to work as a prostitute every now and then.

Once again, it was found that the cause of death was a series of gunshot wounds to the head, consistent with the other murders. The murderer was executing his victims; these were clean and targeted shots. He was aiming and aiming well. The head and the heart seemed to be his main objectives, though it was apparent that some shots to the arms and shoulders were a result of defensive wounds. It didn't matter. He still got them in the end.

As the local police began to learn more about Melinda Mercer, a familiar story emerged. She had no ties to Tacoma itself but was something of a drifter. She had worked in Seattle and other places, mostly waitressing but occasionally delving into sex work when money was tight. The man taking the lead on the investigation, Officer Mattheis, was aware of the murders in Spokane. Though he didn't know much about them, he had heard of the string of deaths and noted that the bodies had all been dumped in similar positions. Sparsely populated areas, open spaces – places where the bodies wouldn't be found very quickly – but not usually buried. That they had all died of gunshot wounds rang another bell. He noted these similarities, but stopped short of driving straight up to Spokane with an unsolved murder file in hand.

Elsewhere in the state, Bobby Yates was traveling home. He had spent the weekend out with the National Guard, on one of his regular weekends away. They had been stationed at Fort Lewis, a base near Tacoma. There, Yates had run through a series of air maneuvers in a helicopter, fairly easy work for a man with such experience. Now, he was set to return to Spokane in time for Christmas. Leaving behind one body in Tacoma, he would hardly wait any time at all before he encountered his next victim.

The body of Shawn Johnson was found on the 18th of December, 1997. It was a week before Christmas when the corpse was found by a team of maintenance workers, men who worked at a sewage treatment plant nearby. It was on Hangman Valley Road, very close to the spot where Darla Scott's body had been found a few weeks before. This time, the way in which the body had been left behind was slightly different.

The killer had made no attempt to bury Shawn. While Darla had a hastily dug grave, Shawn was simply thrown on the ground. There was a half-hearted effort to cover the body with leaves and foliage, but it was winter, so there was not much of this around. Because the colder weather helped preserve the body better, the detectives at the scene of this crime had more to work with.

These detectives were the same men who had worked on the other murders in Spokane. Grabenstein was there in no time at all. At first glance, the scene was a lot like the others. That in itself was telling. Once more, there was no sign of a purse, a wallet, any form of identification card, or any money near the body. Again, it seemed as though the body had been brought to the spot in a vehicle and then the killer had driven away into the night.

It didn't take long for the police and the coroner to identify the victim as Shawn Johnson. Again, she was a women involved in sex work in the city of Spokane, specifically around the East Sprague area. It was noted that two plastic bags had been placed over her head. This was not the cause of death, however. They suspected that was because of the two gunshot wounds. Two shots, both to the head. Again, the doctor took swabs from the victim's mouth, anus, and vagina in the hope that the killer might have left some identifiable trace.

Again, the detectives set out on a mission to gather as much evidence as they could about the victim. Again, they came across similar stories from people who didn't really want to talk to them. One of the first leads they came across was from a man who happened to be her drug dealer. He was already quite convinced something bad had happened, even before the police knew about it. Shawn had been a drug user and was in his debt. The dealer was relaxed about this – he knew her, and knew she would work to get him his money. He kept in regular contact with her, hoping her switch from a regular job in a gas station to working as a prostitute wouldn't jeopardize the thousand dollars he was still owed. One day, however, he stopped hearing from her. Knowing she had a car and a family in the city – things that typically anchor people to one spot – he was worried. As it turned out, he was right to be concerned.

The police were easily able to eliminate the man as a suspect as he had been jailed since the 13th of November, well before the last time anyone had seen Shawn alive.

Perhaps the most telling part of the interview with the dealer was how he finished the story. He finished his account of the victim by saying simply that he assumed "the serial killer had gotten to her." Word was starting to spread through certain parts of the city. There was a killer on the loose and he preyed on prostitutes.

The police continued to look into Shawn Johnson's life. What they found was a tragedy writ on a small scale – in the girl's personal journal. Inside, she confessed that all she had ever wanted had been to settle down, to have a family, a home, children, and someone who would treasure her above all others. Instead, her life was filled with drugs and prostitution. Now, it was over.

One of the people the police spoke to was Shannon Johnson. Shawn had a boy named Eric and he had grown up and fallen in love. Eric and Shannon had gotten married the previous October, just two months before Shawn vanished. The last time either Eric or Shannon saw her was at the wedding. At the time, she had been trying to get help with kicking her drug habit. As it had turned out, this was not to be. Shawn Johnson was added to the list of victims, and the search for the killer continued.

Another Death

People were starting to notice. The public's capacity for ignoring and turning a blind eye to vicious crimes should never be underestimated, but – eventually – the reality of the situation will always break through. Even though most Americans would have happily dismissed the spate of murders as an occupational hazard for those involved in the sex trade, there comes a point when the truth must be acknowledged. Somewhere in Spokane, a serial killer was on the loose.

While the media might revel in such a story, this is not true for the police department. Unlike gang related violence or domestic disputes, a serial killer is an entirely different type of homicide. As discussed earlier, the means, the motive, and the opportunity are the three factors detectives focus on when searching for answers. In cases such as this, the motive is often utterly perplexing. Trying to prevent the actions of a man murdering for fun or self-indulgence is almost impossible, and it makes the investigation that much more difficult.

The response from the Spokane police department was to assemble a special task force. This team would be responsible for the pursuit and capture of the man murdering prostitutes in the city. Grabenstein and Ruetsch, two men who had been on the case since the earliest stages were two of the men included. Teaming up with them were detectives from numerous local forces and divisions. This was a county-wide effort with one objective.

The difference between Spokane and some of America's larger cities was visible in the size of the team. When similar killers have emerged in Los Angeles or New York, the teams assembled to tackle the investigation can contain dozens of people. In Spokane, resources were scarce. Rather than sheer man power, it was to be the rock hard determination and refined skills of the detectives that would throw this case wide open. But to get started, they would have to put in the work where it mattered. Without any details about the murderer as of this moment, that meant finding out as much as possible about the victims.

As the number of victims was increasing, it was becoming clear that the lives of these women overlapped to a large extent. They moved in similar social circles, whether that meant sharing drug dealers or sharing customers. They knew one another, would often spot each other when out working on the streets. As the police began to build up a clearer picture of one girl's life, it began to inform their idea of the community as a whole.

Among the girls on the street, the fear was becoming real. Even before the police had formally acknowledged the existence of a serial killer, the sex workers down in East Sprague had developed their suspicions. Rumors and stories spread like wildfire. Was it someone they knew? Did the killer drive one of the cars they were all familiar with? Was it a regular customer? Was it one of the cops? Was it one them, a member of the clique who had gone mad? Everyone became a suspect.

Girls had to rely on their instincts. Balancing the need to make money with the need to stay alive, they had to judge each and every client on the merits of the immediate situation. Could they trust the man? Did he seem strange? Just how much did she really need this bit of cash? Survival was the main aim. That's why so many stuck to the streets. While there is also the possibility for sex workers to advertise privately and then travel to meet clients (especially easy in the age of the internet), the street offers some degree of protection. In East Sprague, someone was always watching. There was a kind of safety in numbers and the fact that the client had to drive up to the girl gave the latter some kind of vetting power. She could judge a client and refuse, if she was so inclined.

For all the protection of the street, there is no escaping the fact that it invites an inherent conflict with the law. The street is a public place and the cops were patrolling at all times. Whereas the police would normally play a constant cat and mouse game with the girls by arresting them, fining them, and then turning them back out onto the streets, these measures were now being put aside until the killer was caught. The police were keeping an ear close to the ground, willing to hear reports from anyone about people who had gone missing or had not been seen in a while.

They created a list. Because of the nature of the community in question, it wasn't uncommon for people to vanish suddenly and abruptly. People would move in and out of the community without much warning. At this time, however, disappearing suddenly could mean a fate far worse than meeting a new romantic interest and leaving the city. The list the police compiled contained names such as Sunny Oster, Shawn McClenahan, Linda Maybin, and Laurie Wason. All four women were known to work as prostitutes. None of them had been seen in a while.

Rather than waiting for the bodies to appear, the detectives decided to take the initiative. They began to investigate the missing girls before their corpses appeared on the street. They asked friends and family for more information, as well as putting out public messages which asked people in the city whether they had seen any of the girls in question.

Sunny Oster had been reported missing on Christmas Eve, 1997. She had traveled to Spokane to get help from a drug rehabilitation facility. After her family had not heard from her in some time, they phoned the police. Given the time of year, people were starting to get concerned about family members.

These fears were made worse when, on the 26th of December, two more bodies were discovered. Laurie Wason and Shawn McClenahan were found dead in Spokane. Already on the list of missing women the detectives were working from, it was becoming clear that the killer remained a step ahead of his prey and his pursuers. But there was still some debate over whether these two women were victims of the serial killer. According to many people on the street, they were known as snitches, police informants who could well have been killed for talking to the authorities.

In this instance, the overlaps between some of the circles were even more apparent. McClenahan had worked at the same escort agency as Darla Scott and both were known as police informants. Linda Maybin, another name on the missing list, was also known to work for the same people. Convictions that had stemmed from the evidence given by McClenahan had resulted in five years for one drug dealer, the evidence of which was written in the court records. Darla Scott had even lived in that same drug dealer's house at one point. To the detectives, the web of interactions was growing increasingly complicated.

But the killer sliced through the web with apparent ease. He didn't seem to care about who was an informant or who lived where. While Bobby Yates was certainly not a regular member of the criminal underworld in Spokane, the way in which he targeted three women who were so closely associated got people talking. Among the community, people were sure the three missing women were deliberately chosen for the way in which they had snitched, stolen, and ripped people off in the past.

While those on the streets began to suspect anyone who might have known the girls personally, the police had a suspect list that stretched into the thousands. This meant the number of blood samples being taken was astronomical, with each sample being tested by the lab and cross referenced against any clues found at any of the scenes. Most of these samples, taken from clients and associates, were given up willingly.

Shawn McClenahan had been seen on Christmas Eve. Just before 6:00 in the evening, she had been spotted by a man who had seen her crying in the parking lot of a food store. She was visibly upset. Despondent, she explained to the man – a casual acquaintance – about her life, about her desperation to kick her drug habit. She seemed determined to get into a methadone program to help her quit heroin. When she was feeling better, the two parted ways. Shawn promised to phone the man later that evening. The call never came.

Her body was found two days later, stuffed into a gully in a wooded part of Spokane County. Lying next to her was Laurie Wason. The man who found the bodies was Rick Dullanty, an attorney who lived in the area. He had been out for a walk with his son, still very much in the festive spirit. The two had spotted legs, clad in a pair of jeans, protruding from a pile of sodden leaves. It was 2:00 in the afternoon. An hour later, Detective Ruetsch was rushing to the scene.

The gully was a manmade affair. It was a ditch, dug to help with water runoff and to prevent erosion. It served as a makeshift grave, helping to hide the body from plain sight. It was quickly apparent that this was not just one body. While a pair of legs were pointing out towards the west, another limb was pointing in the opposite direction. Looking closely, the detective realized that one of these half-hidden legs was missing a foot.

Both of the corpses seemed to have been in the ditch for quite a while. By now, they were covered in the branches, twigs, leaves, and other natural debris that piled up in the countryside. A recent snowfall of about half an inch covered the ground. With more snow set to fall that evening, the police had to work fast. With daylight fading, they took as many photos as possible and then covered the entire ditch with a sheet of tarpaulin. With guards posted at the scene, the task force assembled to find out what they could.

The next day, things became clearer. The leaves and debris that had been found on top of the bodies were incongruent with the area – they had come from somewhere else. The leaves, twigs, and other items seemed to have been taken from the garbage, regular garden waste that had been brought in from somewhere else and used to hide the bodies. Samples were taken in the hope they might be matched to a particular yard or area. This combination of plants might be from the killer's own garden and might form a kind of horticultural fingerprint that could be used in identification. One of the detectives, a keen gardener himself, personally set about the task and went so far as to create a cheat sheet for the rest of the team, telling them what plants to watch out for when interviewing suspects.

Publically, there was a refusal from the police to attribute the new murders to the same killer. Privately, however, the detectives' minds were already linking together the dead women and the man who had killed the others. There was evidence to justify this. As before, both victims had been shot with a .25 caliber handgun, and it looked like both had been dumped into the ditch at the same time.

But the murders were not the only ones discovered in Spokane that week. Earlier, reports had come in that the bodies of two men had been found. Both had died in shooting incidents. Though the cause of death appeared to be similar, it was impossible to relate them to the murder of the prostitutes with any certainty. Still, it raised questions in the mind of the public and the police. Was the killer branching out?

The police treated the murders with the same degree of interest, and investigated. Though the ties were not so clear, there were connections. For example, Linda Maybin was known to have bought drugs from a certain house in North Spokane several weeks before her body was found. Peter Peterson was murdered a few weeks later, following a similar fate to his brother, who had been murdered back in 1991. As it happened, the man who had murdered Peterson's brother happened to have stayed in the same house where Linda was buying her drugs. It was likely a coincidence, a happenstance resulting from the smaller size of the city and the respectively smaller size of its criminal underworld. But the police did not have the privilege of being so sure. They had to treat all of the murders with the same degree of potential connectedness.

The stories of many of the victims were so similar. Whenever the detectives spoke to the grieving families, they often heard the same kinds of memories. Laurie Wason and Shawn McClenahan had both been recovering drug addicts. At various times, they had been clean. Both of their families hoped the women were on the verge of kicking the habit once and for all. But, with both women having turned back to sex work, the moment had passed. The murders caused unbearable pain amongst the families, grieving for daughters, sisters, mothers, and wives. Stories of addiction, desperation, and prostitution seemed to affect every one of the victims. It's hard to imagine a more despondent and disenfranchised demographic of people that the killer could have targeted.

The autopsy provided similar ratification that these murders were connected. As well as the gunshot wounds and the way in which the bodies had been dumped, there was the presence of the plastic bags, which had been noticed several times now. They now turned their attention to comparing the bags.

Both Laurie and Shawn had their heads covered by three plastic bags. Removing those on Shawn's head, detectives noted where they came from. The first, the outermost bag, came from Safeway and seemed to be fairly plain. The middle bag was even plainer, being entirely devoid of advertising. The innermost bag, the one closest to the dead girl's skin, came from Kmart. It was a special bag, featuring an advertising campaign based on the characters from Sesame Street. The cheeriness of the puppets clashed with the gravity of the situation.

In Laurie's case, the detectives found a similarly eclectic mix of bags. The outermost bag this time came from a Shopko store, a national retail chain. Inside was a paper towel, folded in half. It wasn't much, but it might have been a clue. It was noted and deemed worthy of testing. The remaining two bags were both the same, coming from Albertsons. The bags gave the police little to work with, but they were getting to the stage where even the tiniest detail would be an improvement.

Once the bags were removed, the coroner looked closely at the bullet wounds. Both women had been shot twice in the head, with two bullets recovered from inside their skulls on both occasions. Using forensic lighting technology, the clothing of the victims was examined and a number of envelopes were filled with testable hairs and fibers. While lab reports would later indicate that some of these were actually cat hairs, it demonstrated the extent to which even the tiniest detail was being subjugated to a huge barrage of testing.

One thing was clear just from looking at the corpses: Laurie Wason's body had been dead a lot longer. Though they had been picked up at the same time in the same place, Wason's rate of decomposition was much higher. It raised new questions in the minds of the detectives. If the killer was dumping the bodies at the same time, then it seemed obvious that he had killed them earlier and elsewhere. But this new evidence made them question just how long before the body was dumped was the victim killed? Had the killer kept the corpse for days, or even weeks? If so, where was he storing them? Without much progress being made, the questions were piling up quicker than the bodies.

A Mounting Investigation

One of the biggest challenges facing the task force was understanding the mind of the suspect. The detectives had all worked the crime beat for many years, but the crimes they were used to dealing with almost always had a clear, definitive objective. Material gain, a crime of passion, revenge: these were crimes where it was quickly clear why someone would do such a thing, commit a particular act. But in this instance, trying to empathize with the killer, to get inside his shoes, was proving to be impossible.

Often, in situations such as this, the tendency is to try and find a motive and to come up with scenarios, which may become increasingly unlikely. This was the case many years previously in Walla Walla. The murders of Susan Savage and Patrick Oliver seemed to have been senseless acts of violence, but that didn't stop the investigators from discussing theories of international assassinations and drug conspiracies. Alternatively, when other avenues of investigation have been exhausted, police may decide the act was the work of an insane person, and move on. That may have been the case in Walla Walla, but with the murders continuing, that wasn't an option in Spokane.

The detectives were struggling. There was an increased amount of pressure from the public and the press to catch the killer, and they had nothing to go on. The police were hoping the killer would eventually trip himself up, and make an error somewhere which would be the big breakthrough. How else could the task force otherwise identify the man in question?

That's not to say they were idle. Even if their work was not turning up many leads, the detectives were working harder than ever before, relentlessly tracking down all the information they could about the victims, acting upon every tip or hunch they came across. With such a long list of potential suspects, they were desperate to eliminate as many people as possible. If the public had any idea just how big the list of suspects was, then they might have realized how daunting a task lay ahead of the task force.

Working with the girls from East Sprague, the police had put together a list of vehicles of interest that had been spotted in or around prostitution areas. The makes and models of these cars were checked, as was the list of gun owners in the city. Occasionally, the people they interviewed might deny having ever been to the bad part of town before, much less having engaged the services of a prostitute. But samples were taken and guns were tested. Few people generated much suspicion among the police, and no one really stood out as noteworthy.

The police were also following up on the plastic bag leads. With a number of different stores being advertised on the sides of the bags, they made a list of corresponding stores around the city and wondered whether that might point them towards any specific area. Even if it led to nothing, it might show them where the killer was getting his plastic bags.

However, the main thing connecting the victims was the street. Specifically, they were all known to have spent time on or near Sprague Avenue. It was a notorious haunt for those searching to acquire the affections of a woman for the night, where anyone driving down the street could easily evaluate and examine the women on offer. The dark lighting and the speed of the cars meant they were pretty much hidden themselves. As December passed and January of 1998 began, the investigation was making slow progress.

By the 6th of January, attentions had turned again to the list of missing women. In addition to the women who had been reported missing recently, the police were going back further and further in the files. Women such as Denise Raye Holmes, Jessica Fitzgerald, Sheila Burnette, and (most recently) Brandy Mitchell had not been seen in months. The fact that these women had not been confirmed to be dead meant that they couldn't really be considered as part of the investigation. For example, on the 8th of January, investigators were able to confirm that Brandy Mitchell, at least, was alive and well. For the others, no one could draw any conclusions.

The focus was switched back to the here and now; they could carry on eliminating their suspects. One by one, people were called into the station for questioning. Many underwent lie detector, or polygraph, tests. When the test suggested the person was not the killer, or they had an alibi, or they were able to demonstrate their innocence in some other way, the task force removed that suspect from the list. It was a slow process.

By the middle of January, however, it was clear help was required. With the local police struggling due to a lack of experience in catching a serial killer, federal help was required. The FBI were due to arrive in Spokane on the 20th of January and lend their skills and talents to the ongoing investigation. The day before, a huge church service was held for the murdered women. Ostensibly dedicated to the eighteen women who had been murdered in the city since the mid-1980s, it was a demonstration of solidarity with a part of society usually forgotten or outright ignored. With so many people in attendance, the task force decided to film the event using small, hidden cameras, just in case there was anything of note. They would review the footage later.

When the FBI arrived, their first and perhaps most important move was to put together a profile. The task force had been struggling to get to know the killer, but the FBI's experience in dealing with similar criminals across the country meant they were better equipped to make a psychological evaluation of the murderer. They presented profile this to the task force and it was met with a tepid response. The detectives felt it contained very few specific details, and decided it would be of little help in their work.

The profile was broad. According to the FBI, the killer was likely a white male. His age was probably between 20 and 40. Socially, he might be something of a loner. That was it.

The FBI, knowing this was not the most complete of profiles, advised the team that it was not meant to be a definitive identification of the killer. Rather, it was meant to act as a background piece of information rather than offering immediate direction. Unfortunately, the description could be applied to the majority of men in Spokane, most of whom had never even thought about killing anyone. It was with some disappointment that the profile was tossed on the pile.

But the FBI's profile was not the only one in existence. For reasons of their own or another, outside organizations had also put together their own profiles. They often described him as a street person, or someone with an existing criminal record. Another stated that the killer likely knew his victims and moved in their same social circles. Some described him as part of the terrain or part of the environment down in East Prague. Others were more specific, that he suggesting he would be a pimp or a junkie. While there were elements of truth in nearly all the profiles, many of the details contradicted one another. Without the benefit of hindsight, the detectives didn't know which details were the correct ones. While the profiles were consulted, they could not be relied upon.

If there was good news, it came in the form of a sudden slew of tips and information. People were now more willing to share their thoughts and ideas with the police. Typically, the relationship between the police and the sex workers in the city was frosty at best. Arrests and fines usually resulted from any conversation between such parties. Now, however, everyone seemed to have a shared goal in mind – to catch the serial killer.

But the sudden surge of information had a downside as well. The police found they were being dragged from pillar to post, visiting people all over the city who claimed to know something. These people were often prostitutes themselves, or drug users who occupied the same streets. They might have known the victims through shared associates, having done drugs with them or spent time living in the same house. It meant many of the reports were conflicting and often of dubious quality. Sometimes, it seemed as though the potential witness had an axe to grind with a particular person and wanted them arrested as a serial killer, even if this was not the case. Elsewhere, reports from one witness were immediately contradicted by reports from another. The task force found that attempting to find the kernels of truth in these stories was like trying to find a needle in a haystack.

Things became more complicated as the weeks dragged on. On Sunday, the 8th of February, another body was found. A member of the public had been out walking on the roads to the west of Spokane County. When they spotted something strange, the police were called.

At the time, the police were unwilling to confirm that the body was definitively related to the ongoing serial killer investigation. Over the course of the next few days, however, it became clear this was the case. The presence of three plastic bags around the victim's head was a major indication, as was the fact that a single gunshot wound to the head had been the cause of death.

The position of the body was also in line with the other cases. Out walking dogs and horses, the person who made the discovery had been intrigued when one of the dogs had taken an interest in a cluster of trees situated by the roadside. Believing she could see some clothes by the road, she looked closely. When she saw the foot, it was clear to her the police would need to be called.

The crime scene demonstrated just why the task force were reluctant to immediately add this body to the list of victims. The body had clearly been in place for a long time, and the decomposition made even determining the gender of the victim very difficult. Grabenstein was called to the scene anyway and, by the time he arrived, it was already getting dark.

The body had been dumped into a ditch on the western side of the road. It had been placed face down, with the right arm tucked beneath the body and the left arm stretching out to the west. Accordingly, the left arm had been almost stripped of flesh, and most of the hand was missing. Animals had gotten to the body. The skin showed signs of putrefaction and the decay resulting from exposure to the elements. Apart from the damage to the left arm, however, the rest of the body seemed to be remarkably intact.

The body was still wearing clothes. Grey jeans and a black top were visible, though the sweater had been damaged along the left arm. The victim's shoes and socks were missing. As might be expected, a plastic bag had been placed over the head and it looked like the killer had made an effort to place weeds, grass, and other vegetation on top of the body. This was not to say it had been buried, but more that the body had been covered, perhaps some of the covering having been shifted by weather or animals.

Once again, major clues were absent. There were no shoeprints, no tire marks, and nothing apart from the hoof prints, dog tracks, and the traces left behind by the woman who had discovered the body.

It was around this time that the family members of a number of the victims held a press conference. Through the press, they pleaded with the still-unknown killer to stop what he was doing. They begged the man to turn himself in and to end the suffering of the families. Nothing happened.

By the 10th of February, the results from the crime scene were starting to filter back to the task force. An identification was made, confirming the victim was one of the women on the missing persons list, Sunny Oster. The family were notified. They had already been fearing the worst.

A member of Sunny's family hatched a bizarre plan to help the investigation. Dorothy Werttemberger, a cousin of the deceased, was angry about the murder. She resolved to do something about it and went to the police with an idea. She would follow in the footsteps of her cousin, retracing her movements as best she could, right up until the last time Sunny was seen. During this time, she would carry a GPS tracker. Essentially working as a prostitute, she was willing to put herself in harm's way if it meant the killer could be caught. Dorothy's reasoning was that the killer might repeat his actions, pick her up, and the authorities would be lead straight to their suspect.

Dorothy was not new to innovative methods of investigation. Before coming up with this plan, she had visited a psychic, a man whom she hoped would be able to track the killer using supernatural forces. She visited Jeff Reynolds, a medium who had supposedly worked on the investigation into Ted Bundy, another serial killer. Reynolds had pretty much retired from these 'distance readings' and had started writing about crime instead.

In talking to Reynolds, Dorothy heard another profile of the killer. According to the psychic, the man they wanted suffered from a sexual dysfunction which prevented him from getting an erection. He could only satisfy himself when the victim was already dead.

Reynolds said he could see a location in his mind's eye, a kind of workshop or a machine shop where the killer spent time with his victims. Once he was finished, the killer would take the body out and dump it. That he poured garbage and debris on top of the women was not so much an attempt to hide the bodies as it was a final act of humiliation.

Reynolds gave Dorothy one final warning. He told her the task force might not appreciate her outlandish ideas. Already deep into the investigation, they might not enjoy demands from an enthusiastic amateur. Dorothy decided not to talk to the authorities about her conversation with Reynolds. She didn't want to hinder the process of catching her cousin's killer.

Instead, the task force were using their own strange methods to try and make progress. They engaged a helicopter to fly over the sites known to have been used by the killer to dump bodies. The aircraft was fitted with thermal imaging equipment. If there were any other bodies in the area, it was thought they might show up, because the decomposition process would give off heat. If the killer was using the same sites repeatedly, there might be as-yet uncovered bodies scattered around. Given that it was approaching late February, the cold ground would contrast with the dead girls and provide the police with a new line of investigation.

There was another theory that they might be able to lure the killer out into the open. Several experts on the matter had suggested it was not uncommon for serial killers to return to the grave sites of their victims. By keeping a close eye on who showed up at the burial sites, the police might be able to get a glimpse of the man. In a similar fashion, the vigils and memorial services held for the victims were closely watched, because the killer might take an interest in such events.

The task force hoped to combine the two ideas. They could hold a new event in memory of the victims, this time basing it at one of the dumping sites. The event would be heavily publicized and broadcast by the media. The police were certain their man would take an interest.

By the end of March, things were not looking much better. In all, the department had received close to a thousand tips from various sources. Chasing down all these leads was impossible, but increased manpower and a better budget meant that progress was being made. By the first of April, however, it was shown again what a difficult process this was. Another body was found.

A Dead End

The body was found on the 1st of April. By this point, the routine was almost second nature to the task force. It was in almost the same spot where killer had dumped Laurie Wason and Shawn McClenahan. A perimeter was set up and the crime scene investigation could begin once again.

The body had been found by a couple and their child who had been walking along Fourteenth Street that afternoon. They had noticed a strange shape, something which appeared to be a partially clothed person just to the side of the road, at the bottom of another ditch. They decided not to touch anything but to phone the police. Word about the serial killer had spread enough through the city, and people were starting to know what to expect.

The new site was roughly fifty feet from the spot where the other two bodies had been abandoned, in the same drainage ditch. The body appeared to be wearing blue jeans and tennis shoes, which were the first things visible. Again, there had been an attempt to cover up the body but not bury it. The killer had used leaves and grass to hide the victim. In the detective's opinion, the debris had been thrown down on top of the body from the roadside, likely after the body was thrown from the car. In all likelihood, the covering would have been enough to hide the body completely at first, but the weather had moved enough to reveal the corpse.

There were also scraps of torn clothing scattered about the site. The biggest of these was a large piece of red material, seemingly the same sweater from which all of the smaller pieces had been ripped. The pieces could have been scattered by a scavenging animal, it was thought. Other evidence was scarce.

The police found an empty whiskey bottle, a soft drink bottle, and other pieces of assorted garbage. It wasn't clear where they had come from. Additionally, there were tire impressions left behind by vehicles which had pulled over to the side of the road, at least one of which appeared to be fresh.

When the body was taken in for the autopsy, the killer's usual handiwork was found. The head had been wrapped in a pair of plastic bags and there was a bullet hole in the skull. It wasn't long before the body was identified as that of Linda Daveys, one of the missing women. The family were informed.

One of the unique clues taken from this scene was a condom. It had been found during the autopsy, lodged between the cheeks of the victim's buttocks, an area that had been exposed when the seat of the jeans rotted away. It was pink and it was used. Immediately, it was sent for testing.

Having a potential DNA sample of the suspect was a big clue. The information, while it might not match up against any other DNA records held by the state, would reveal a great deal. This included any prescription medications the suspect might be using, any illegal drugs they might have ingested, as well as any other tiny details that could be taken from the semen sample.

It was a long shot but – for the first time in ages – the task force seemed to have a rock solid clue. They could test this sample, use it to compare and contrast, and perhaps even hunt down a potential suspect. One downside, however, is that such extensive testing might well lead to the destruction of the evidence. If this happened, then it would amount to a dead end. There was an inherent risk in testing the condom which was not only old and used, but had been exposed to the elements for so long. If the wrong tests were done, then the investigators might lose their chance of finally tracing the suspect. Accepting this, they choose to carry out as many tests as possible.

Elsewhere in the city, a woman named Rita Jones was driving home in her new car. For years, she had dreamed of owning a Corvette. Now, finally, she had realized that dream. It was secondhand, sure, but that didn't diminish her pleasure as she relished the feel of the steering wheel. It was white, and she enjoyed seeing it in the shop windows as she drove past.

As well as admiring herself behind the wheel, Rita was thinking back on the deal she had just made. It seemed fair enough, just under $9,000 for a car like this. Of course, she hadn't mentioned it was her dream vehicle. No need to bring that into the negotiation. The man she had bought it from seemed nice enough. His name had been Robert Yates and, according to his story, he had owned the car for years. That didn't matter now, though, it was her car. She should enjoy it.

But there was a problem. The car was beautiful; it had been cared for over the years, the owner clearly knowing how to maintain such a vehicle. But a car such as this should be stored in a garage. To keep it on the street would just be asking for trouble, but Rita didn't own a garage. Luckily for her, a friend had offered to help out. As it happened, the friend – a relative, actually – worked for the police department, in their property room, and they had offered to help her out. It seemed like the ideal solution, Rita thought as she drove her new car home. She couldn't wait to get it out and really get to know her new white Corvette.

In an effort to catch the killer, the task force were trying everything. That included the carefully observed memorial service, where they hoped to lure the killer out. It was held near Hangman Valley Road. There were undercover officers lurking around the place, disguised as homeless people and dog walkers. Others were camouflaged to look like plant life, and they lay motionless in the undergrowth for twelve hours at a time.

They even set up motion detectors and photographed the license plates of any passing car.

The memorial service went ahead. It included a few words from the sheriff, though many family members declined to take part. Leaving behind memorials, including flower wreaths and photographs of the dead girls, the police hoped the killer might return to the scene to take a trophy. They watched for three days afterward, but no one came.

As the investigation dragged on, it seemed as though the killer had noticed the task force's increasingly desperate measures to catch him. The slew of murders slowed down. By June, they seemed to have stopped. Even though the police were still working hard to catch the man, there had not been a verified instance of the killer striking in a long time. Perhaps inevitably, public interest waned.

Needing new information, the task force continued to check every possible lead. One such avenue of investigation involved compiling lists of all the owners of any vehicle closely associated with the crimes. This included a list of white Corvette owners. This list was then crosschecked against another list of those people who had been stopped in areas associated with prostitution. One of the names that came up was Robert Lee Yates junior. But he was not alone. This entry was just one of many generated by the task force. It was added to the pile.

Soon, the public's attention was awakened again. This time, it was with the discovery of the body of Melody Murfin, a missing person who was known to have associated with the other victims in the past. Just as people were starting to feel safe again, the killer struck. It didn't take long for this latest victim to be verified as being by the same killer.

On the 3rd of July, Michelyn Derning vanished. Michelyn had previously been a secretary but had found herself plunging further and further into the Spokane underworld. When she didn't show up for a trip with a friend, she was reported missing. It was another name added to the list of potential victims.

The body was found in a vacant parking lot. She was stripped bare, and the killer had scattered a few branches and the cover from an old hot tub on top. Having fallen victim to drugs, homelessness and prostitution in the past, she fit the template of the other victims. Just as before, when inspecting the scene, the detectives found no purse or identification. There was a gunshot wound in her head, from a .25 caliber handgun.

Even after months had passed, the killer had hardly altered a thing. At this point, yet another body taught the task force very little about their target. The discovery of the body ran along the same lines as every other instance. As soon as the body was identified, they called the family with the bad news.

What they didn't know at the time was that the location was significant. The vacant lot at North 218 Crestline was right next to Pantrol, a business which happened to employ Bobby Yates. As with all their other crime scene investigations, the detectives went through the list of anyone who might be near the site at any given time. Bobby Yates was interviewed among the Pantrol employees but he did nothing to make himself stand out. He just seemed like a regular guy, an average worker in a long line of average workers. His details were taken and added to the list. At this point, the sheer amount of information relating to the case made it almost impossible to double check the name against previous interactions. For the time being, Bobby Yates slipped through the detectives' grasp once again.

A Living Witness

It was the 1st of August, and for the very first time in the case, a victim was about to escape with her life.

Just after midnight, Christine Smith met the killer. Like many of the other victims, Christine was a prostitute. Like many of the girls working in Spokane, she was worried about the killer on the loose. But she needed the money. When a man drove up alongside her and asked her to get in his van, she outright asked him whether he was the serial killer. Bobby Yates denied it. He was an Army veteran and a father of five. She had nothing to fear, he said.

Christine believed him and got in the vehicle. Almost immediately, Yates encouraged her to perform oral sex. Christine obliged but spent the next seven minutes trying to help her client achieve an erection. With her attentions focused on this, she never saw the man reaching around behind her. She didn't hear anything, just experienced a sharp, sudden pain in her head. Christine had been shot.

But she wasn't dead. The pain might have been extreme, but the girl had somehow – miraculously – survived. Her first thought was that the client must have hit her, annoyed at his sexual failures. She could hear Yates demanding his money back and could hear him shouting at her. But she was in shock. Dazed, confused, she could feel the blood dripping from her head wound.

It was a fight to stay conscious. Battling, Christine got up and scrambled out the door. She ran, going as fast as she possibly could, straight to the nearby rehab center. It was one of the few places open at that time of night, one of even fewer places who were not dismayed to see one of the sex workers come in off the street. She was bleeding from the head, and the rehab employees could see Christine was in trouble. They called an ambulance.

But there was no real indication that Christine had been attacked by the serial killer. It could just have easily have been another attempted robbery or a falling out between a girl and her client. These frequently ended in violence, the clients feeling immune from protection given how infrequently the girls went to the cops with any issues. Once again, it seemed as though Bobby Yates had gotten away with it.

In the middle of September, Bobby Yates had another run-in with the law. Pulled over by a cop, he was asked whether he would be able to provide them with a DNA sample. It was a fairly innocuous question, something asked of many people who interacted with the Spokane police at the time. Yates refused. He claimed that such a thing was "too extreme," not something the police should request of a family man such as he was. Thinking little of it, the officer allowed Yates to go about his business.

The task force was continuing on in spite of this, not realising how close they had come on numerous occasions. They were still searching for missing girls. In late August, there had been some commotion when a family dog had returned home with a chuck of human scalp in its mouth. After an extended search, the police gave up. The dog could have found it anywhere. Melody Murfin's killer still eluded the police and they struggled to make any real advancements in the case.

Another body was found in October. It belonged to Connie LaFontaine Ellis. She was found in a ditch in Tacoma. The scene bore all the hallmarks of the same killer. The name was added to the investigation, the Tacoma detectives resolving to work with their Spokane counterparts. The search continued.

On the 10th of November, Bobby Yates had another close call with the police. Picking up a prostitute named Jennifer in Spokane, he agreed to a fee of $20 in exchange for oral sex. As they drove off, the flash of police lights halted them. As the officer approached, Jennifer invented a story. Tell them I'm your friend's daughter, she told Yates, and that you're here to give me a lift. She corroborated the story when the officer asked and, once again, the police let Bobby go. If he had been planning on murdering Jennifer that night, then it appeared as though he changed his mind. He let her go.

Two days later, however, Bobby Yates heard a knock on his front door. When he answered, he stood face to face with the Spokane police. They were there to respond to claims of a domestic dispute in the house. Bobby had been fighting with his teenage daughter and, in the course of the argument, had threatened her physically. The police agreed to let him off the attendant assault charge if he kept quiet and obeyed the law. There was no mention of the Spokane serial killer as Yates waved the police off.

The task force had been working for over a year now. During that time, they had not been able to prevent the murder of a string of women. Of the three thousand tips they had received, the detectives had managed to follow up on about half of them. Still, the investigators remained confident and insisted that they were making progress.

While they had not gone public with their progress, they were telling the truth. For around six months, they had the killer's DNA on file, and a likely palm print as well. This had been recovered from one of the plastic bags, using a technique one of the investigators learned about while watching the Discovery Channel. The DNA had come from the swabs taken from numerous victims, as well as the used condom. While it would be useful when verifying a suspect, they still needed a suspect's DNA against which to test their sample.

The killer seems to have been spooked. Perhaps the recent run-ins with the law and the failed attack on Christine made him nervous enough to dissuade him from further murders at the moment. For months, no new bodies were found.

Perhaps this was because Bobby Yates was having his own problems. Work trouble at Pantrol meant he needed a new job, fast. Searching around, he found temporary work with Kaiser Aluminum in December of 1998. It was tough, physical work, usually taken on by men much younger than Bobby. But it didn't seem to be enough. Linda Yates noted at the time that money was short. When looking at the bank statements, frequent cash withdrawals by Bobby were a major drain. When she brought up the subject, he shut her down and told her to get a job. She had no idea he had been spending money on crack cocaine and prostitutes.

By this time, Bobby Yates's sexual frustrations were becoming a real issue for him. He had sometimes experienced impotence over the years, but the matter was becoming desperate. He had mentioned to Linda the idea of trying Viagra, but she played off the problems as the two of them simply being tired. But Bobby couldn't let the idea go. Sex seemed to become an obsession for him.

Soon, Linda began to take extra notice of her husband's credit card receipts. It included motels rooms she had no idea about. Bobby claimed he used the motel's hot tub to soothe his muscles after work. He never mentioned the prostitutes. Linda thought Bobby was having an affair. She had no idea of the real scale of the truth.

The real clue should have come at the end of 1999. Without anyone in the family knowing, Bobby Yates brought home a corpse. It was Melody Murfin. Taking great care to hide his tracks, Bobby buried it in the family yard, just beneath the bedroom window. For months, no one would even realize it was there.

Throughout the first few months of 1999, Bobby kept quiet. The silence was maintained for weeks, then months, and then almost a year. Throughout the year, the signs of any serial killer activity seemed to dry up. But the task force continued to operate.

Despite some internal power struggles in the police department, the detectives remained committed to finding the killer. Even if he had gone to ground, that simply gave them the chance to track down the backlog of leads they had. That was why, on the 15th of September, 1999, they brought in Bobby Yates for questioning.

Bobby seemed to be on edge. He was sweating as he answered the detectives' questions. They asked him whether he ever hired prostitutes. He admitted it. At least, he admitted to visiting prostitutes when stationed in Germany with the Army. In Spokane, he had never done such a thing.

The detectives asked for alibis and noted that – on two significant dates – Bobby came up short. They brought up the report from the traffic incident to him. Reading it, Bobby corrected them. It hadn't been a white Camaro. It had been a white Corvette, he said. This started alarm bells ringing.

When the interview was coming to a close, the police asked Bobby for a blood sample. He refused. While this is the right of any citizen, it certainly added to the police's growing suspicions. Following up on the incident, the police got in touch with

Jennifer, the prostitute Yates had been pulled over with. She admitted she had lied.

Three days later, Bobby Yates left a message on the answering machine for Detective Grabenstein. Sorry, he said, but he would not be providing a blood sample. The police were especially interested in those who were reluctant to do so, with so many men willing to eliminate themselves from suspicion. When they put this together with other factors such as the Corvette, the police began to turn their focus on Bobby Yates.

But there were problems. Budget issues and a lack of progress meant the task force was losing men, and those who remained were working so hard their health was suffering. They went into the 1999 Christmas period unsure whether the task force would even exist the next year.

In January, with morale at an all-time low, the team finally tracked down the white Corvette. They had found Rita Jones and asked permission to check over the car for forensic evidence. She agreed and the police checked every inch of the vehicle. This resulted in a number of recovered hairs and fiber samples. These were sent for analysis. They also discovered that the carpets had been changed numerous times.

While they waited for the results from the car, the team began to check out Bobby Yates's background. They interviewed his former employers at Pantrol and discovered the company had given him permission to use a number of their vehicles. Some of these matched descriptions from prostitutes in Sprague. Investigations continued.

It was the 5th of April when the forensics lab returned its first match. They had examined fibers taken from the white Corvette, and matched them to one found on Jennifer Joseph's (Jennifer Kim's) body. They were the same. It was the team's first major breakthrough after years of searching. Immediately, they put Bobby Yates under round-the-clock surveillance.

Plans were already forming about how best to arrest their suspect. The killer hadn't struck in months so it seemed unlikely they were going to catch him in the act.

As it happened, the Spokane County sheriff was out of town on that day. He happened to be friends with his equivalent in Walla Walla. The two were spending time together and, when news of the potential arrest came through, the men chatted about the subject. When it came up that the suspect might be from Walla Walla, memories began to ease into motion. Eventually, the Oliver and Savage murders would be linked to the arrest of Bobby Yates. The fact that so many of the dates lined up made both men excited. It increased the chances of conviction.

The white Corvette was seized and subjected to even more intense examination. Blood flakes were found on the interior and a missing button from Jennifer Joseph's blouse was discovered under the passenger seat. It had been there for years. When the blood was tested, it was a match with blood taken from Jennifer's parents.

Bobby, unaware of the police's sudden breakthrough, was having troubles of his own. Linda had once again confronted him about a $600 difference between her expectations of their bank balance and the reality. To her surprise, Bobby broke down in tears. He told her that he had a problem and that he had spent a great deal of the family's money buying gifts for everyone. It was a bald-faced lie. As was the story about a gambling problem soaking up the family funds. As Bobby cried, Linda reached the end of her tether. She walked out of the room. There was an impending sense of dread in the household, though she didn't know the true scale of the situation.

By the 17th of April, the police had been planning the arrest for days. The Yates house was staked out and everyone seemed to be sleeping. They had watched Bobby enter the home the night before and at 6:00 the next morning, they watched him leave for work. They followed.

As planned, two uniformed officers signaled for Yates to pull over. He did so, parking in a church lot. Within minutes, the task force, led by Detective Rick Grabenstein, arrived on the scene. The suspect was removed from the car and placed in handcuffs. Told that he was under arrest on suspicion of murder, Yates hardly seemed concerned at all.

What followed was a long process. Immediately upon being brought in, Robert was subjected to hours of questioning. Meanwhile, Linda had received a phone call saying that her husband hadn't shown up for work. Suspecting he was off at the motel, Linda drove to the address on the credit card statement. Finding no one there, she went for a coffee. It was then the police approached her and explained the situation. Linda and the rest of the family were prevented from returning home. At the police's expense, they were put up in a nearby hotel. The police even collected the family cats, and were on hand at every moment to make sure the family was ok. In previous cases involving serial killers, it was common for the family to have no idea about the reality of the situation. That certainly seemed to be the case here.

Robert Lee Yates junior was arrested under suspicion of up to eighteen murders. The police were reticent to give too much away to the press, in case the conviction didn't go through, but they were quietly confident of making their accusations stick. Sniffer dogs checked out the Yates home and hotlines were set up. A press release was drafted and people were welcomed to submit any information that they might have on Bobby Yates. Gradually, the case was being built against the suspect.

Thankfully for the Spokane police department, they had the right man. Robert Lee Yates junior was the man responsible for murdering many women. Now, the police had him behind bars.

Conclusion

Of course, there is a huge difference between suspecting a person of committing a crime and proving it in a court of law. Luckily for the police department, they had overwhelming amounts of evidence. The DNA samples might have been enough to convict most people, but there was also the discovery of the body buried in the yard, and the witness testimonies. Numerous other pieces of evidence were soon put forward.

Eventually, Yates was charged with thirteen counts of murder in the first degree. They suspected he might be involved in even more, but these were the cases the police felt confident about. Besides, it would be more than enough to secure a long prison sentence. In addition, Yates was charged with attempted murder in the first degree when the run-in with Christine became a major part of the case.

Facing this array of charges, Yates and his lawyers agreed to a plea bargain. In order to avoid the death penalty, Yates would confess to the murders. For the prosecution, this avoided a lengthy, costly trial and secured the result they wanted. Yates was sentence to 408 years behind bars.

But that was not the end of the story. The following year, further charges were put forward. Police in Pierce County accused Yates of two additional murders, those of Melinda Mercer and Connie LaFontaine Ellis. They sought the death sentence, and they won. In October of 2002, Yates was sentenced to death by lethal injection. In a strange twist, the existing conviction of 408 years meant that the current sentence would have to be served before the death penalty could be implemented. Technically, Yates would survive.

But Yates appealed anyway. In his defense, his lawyers argued that the plea bargain was meant to include all of the murders in question and that the application of the death penalty in this instance was "freakish ... and random." This appeal was rejected. But it would not be the last.

In 2013, lawyers acting for Yates sent a petition which claimed their client was mentally ill, and they claimed that a condition of severe paraphilic disorder meant that the murders were not Yates's fault.

Yates remains on death row, even though political changes in the state of Washington have led to a move away from the death penalty as a means of punishment. The current Governor has suggested that he might refuse to sign a warrant for capital punishment. In 2015, the Washington Supreme Court rejected the latest appeal against Yates's sentence. As of 2016, Yates remains behind bars, likely to remain there for the foreseeable future.

For a man who terrorized parts of Spokane over an extended period of time, Robert Yates seems to have faded from the public memory. As one of the country's only serial killers to have been caught and remain behind bars, it is strange to some that he is not better known. With pending appeals and court cases, we may never know the real side of events from Yates's perspective. He has not told the police exactly how or where he committed his crimes, and we have no insight into his state of mind or thinking at the time. We may never know the reality behind his actions. Until such a time, we can only guess as to what drove a man to kill so many people.

Further Reading

Barer, B. (2013). *Body count*. New York: Pinnacle.

Berry-Dee, C. (2003). *Talking with serial killers*. London: John Blake.

Cheney, M. and Cheney, M. (2000). *Why*. Lincoln, Neb.: iUniverse.

Morrison, H. and Goldberg, H. (2004). *My life among the serial killers*. Sydney: HarperCollins Publishers.

Moss, J. and Kottler, J. (1999). *The last victim*. London: Virgin.

Vronsky, P. (2004). *Serial killers*. New York: Berkley Books.

Wilson, C. and Seaman, D. (2007). *The serial killers*. London: Virgin.

Cover image credit
By Source (WP:NFCC#4), Fair use, https://en.wikipedia.org/w/index.php?curid=42328191

More Books from Jack Smith

Made in United States
Cleveland, OH
22 March 2025